Marriage Be Hard

Marriage Be Hard

12 CONVERSATIONS TO KEEP YOU LAUGHING, LOVING, AND LEARNING WITH YOUR PARTNER

Kevin Fredericks and Melissa Fredericks

CONVERGENT

NEW YORK

Published in the United States by Convergent Books,
an imprint of Random House, a division of
Penguin Random House LLC, New York.

CONVERGENT BOOKS is a registered trademark and its C colophon is
a trademark of Penguin Random House LLC.

LIBRARY OF CONGRESS CATALOGING-IN-PUBLICATION DATA
Names: Fredericks, Kevin (Comedian), author. | Fredericks, Melissa, author.
Title: Marriage be hard / Kevin Fredericks and Melissa Fredericks.
Description: New York: Convergent, [2022]
Identifiers: LCCN 2022016146 (print) | LCCN 2022016147 (ebook) |
ISBN 9780593240427 (hardcover) | ISBN 9780593240434 (ebook)
Subjects: LCSH: Marriage—Humor.
Classification: LCC PN6231.M3 F37 2022 (print) | LCC PN6231.M3 (ebook) |
DDC 306.8102/07—dc23/eng/20220429
LC record available at https://lccn.loc.gov/2022016146
LC ebook record available at https://lccn.loc.gov/2022016147

Printed in the United States of America on acid-free paper

crownpublishing.com

2 4 6 8 9 7 5 3 1

First Edition

Book design by Edwin Vazquez

Contents

Introduction

This book is called *Marriage Be Hard* for two reasons. The first is that staying married takes some serious work, and everyone needs as much support as they can get. The second reason is that we didn't get that kind of support when the two of us got married eighteen years ago. We grew up churchy, surrounded by opinions about love, sex, and marriage but little concrete advice. At counseling sessions and marriage retreats, it seemed people were selling themselves and their relationships as perfect or nearly perfect while the two of us silently struggled. And social media didn't help either. Instagram can make you feel like every other couple is sailing through this marriage thing without having to put in the work.

Looking back, we see that we were completely in the dark about what it takes to see a marriage through the stuff life throws at you: financial struggles, mental health issues, dream chasing, parenting, and now quarantining. It's easy to get overwhelmed and lost; we did. That's why our podcast, *The Love Hour,* was born. The idea was to create a platform to provide the wisdom, candor, and counsel we wish we'd had when we were newly married.

Kevin:

Wait! Hold up for a sec. Let us take a second to explain what we mean by *churchy*. *Churchy* is the culture of the Black church. It's more than just believing in God or worshipping on Sunday morning. It's the familiar connective tissue that a lot of us experienced as children. It's Sunday school followed by three-hour church services. It's chicken dinners between services and revival on a school night. It's four-hour choir rehearsal and usher practice. Growing up churchy means knowing the all-too-familiar call and response routines:

"God is good all the time."
"And all the time, God is good."

"Won't he do it?"
"Won't he will!"

"I went to a meeting one night and my heart wasn't right."
"But something got a hold of me!"

And of course, those churchy folks had plenty of so-called wisdom about sex. Here are some of the gems they imparted:

- Sex should occur only in the missionary position.
- It's better to marry than to burn. (The actual verse says, "It is better to marry than to burn with passion."[1] In other words, don't torture yourself by not getting married and thus not having sex. But the way it landed for us was "You wanna have sex so bad? Better to get married than burn in hell for having premarital sex.")
- Lay down and be nice. (This is a direct quote from the

first lady of Melissa's church. Translation: When your husband wants sex, you better give it to him.)

And of course, there was the big one: "Don't have sex before marriage." If you grew up Christian, you probably heard this yourself. But no one ever told us *how* not to have sex. And people need to know, because sex is everywhere. You know how much sex was on *Game of Thrones*? *A lot*. What's worse is that your hormones don't care about your religious beliefs or your commitment to your spouse. Your hormones want you to subscribe to OnlyFans. We don't want that for you.

Melissa:

Of course, you could have gone to a Black church your whole life and had an entirely different experience. That's totally fine. This is our experience and the experience of the vast majority of our family and friends. Okay. Back to what we were saying . . .

Churchy people like to talk about everything: the pastor's last service, the praise team, even marriage. But there's a whole world of things you will never hear Christians talking about. Most of all: s-e-x. That's how it was for me. No one discussed sex unless they were telling you all the bad stuff that would happen if you dared enter a sexual relationship before marriage. So I did what they told me to do: I waited until marriage; I went to counseling; I went to marriage enrichment workshops; I attended all the women's Bible studies. But I still felt terrified and unprepared.

In church, in Christian homes, no one shares what they're struggling with. It is common to hear "Look where the Lord has brought me from." It's not so common to hear "Look what the Lord is doing for me right now as I am struggling." Kev and

I have struggled. Our marriage has gone through challenging seasons. I have felt devastatingly alone even when Kevin was right in the next room—and now, eighteen years into our marriage, we're working harder on our relationship than ever before. We pay close attention, we set aside time to talk, we go to therapy, and we deal with issues in our relationship as they arise.

That's my primary reason for this book. On the podcast, we've tackled a wide range of topics, lots of which circle around Christianity and sex and how to reconcile a life that includes both. In one episode, we took a cardinal rule of Christianity—abstinence—and broke it down. We gave our listeners specific advice about how *not* to have sex before marriage. People went crazy. It was as if no one had ever gotten this kind of straight-up advice before.

My initial intention was to serve as a teacher, but more often I ended up being a student. For example, I used to think that sex was a binary thing in a relationship: Men always wanted it and women could do without it. But when we interviewed Dr. Laurie Watson, a relationship counselor and podcast host, I learned that there is such a thing as a higher-desire woman and a lower-desire man. While I was sitting in my chair learning all of this, I said "Wow" out loud into my microphone. I was blown away, and it turned out I wasn't alone. When the episode aired, I received countless emails and DMs from women who thanked me for having a conversation about higher-desire women. They had felt so lonely, thinking there was something wrong with them for wanting more sex than their husbands did. They worried that their husbands weren't attracted to them. Getting feedback like this reminded me daily of the good we were doing on our podcast.

It was a not-so-gentle reminder that we all need constant,

honest conversations *in* our marriage and *about* our marriage. If you and your spouse are going to build a healthy life together, you will need to get comfortable visiting—and revisiting—a whole range of topics together, from infidelity to sex to the way you navigate fights and disagreements. You're even going to have to talk about *talking*. If you've been letting these issues go unvoiced, you're not alone. It's hard to have difficult conversations in the flow of real life. Stopping the busyness of your day with the sole purpose of being honest and vulnerable is not a natural or easy thing. Once again, *marriage be hard*. But putting your relationship on autopilot can lead to even more unpleasant consequences.

These were some of the many lessons we learned by hosting *The Love Hour*. For five years, the show served as our master class for marriage, sex, love, and life. It allowed us the opportunity to sit down with experts in all those fields, and we gained so much knowledge and wisdom. Last year, we brought the show to a close—there is peace in knowing when a task is completed, and we realized that's how we felt about *The Love Hour*. It was time to graduate to the next chapter. This book is our next chapter. It's a chance to reflect in greater depth on conversations we've had with experts and listeners, while exploring many topics we've never discussed openly before. We think of this book as a gift to ourselves and to you: something we all can take with us on our relationship journeys.

Part of our story reads like a Christian fairy tale: high school sweethearts, didn't have sex as teenagers, never sowed any wild oats, never fulfilled exotic desires, and are almost two decades into this marriage. Together, we have gone from prom king and queen to college graduates to parents of adolescents; from broke newlyweds to two fully functional adults with thriving careers. The other part of our relationship would never be discussed on Sundays: the part where we talk openly in public about sex, infidelity, and divorce. Marrying each other was the smartest thing we've ever done, but that doesn't mean every day is a house party. It ain't.

We were best friends who fell in love, and today we are still best friends. But if you think that means it's been a cakewalk for us, you would be wrong. We have had more bumps along the road than we can count, and we're not naïve enough to think all the bumps are behind us. When it comes to all the little things that keep a marriage smooth and clicking, we have gotten it wrong a whole mess of times. We have said the wrong thing to each other, done the wrong thing, and avoided the right thing. We have communicated ineffectively, failed to make our marriage the priority, and fought unfairly.

A lot of our hurdles come from the fact that we are not naturally compatible. In fact, the cliché "opposites attract" is a more accurate depiction of our relationship. Recently, we took a bunch of character assessments and personality tests and learned that we are *complete* opposites. For one, Kevin is a dreamer and Melissa is a realist—and that dynamic was never more obvious than when Kev first decided to chase his dream of becoming a comedian. Around that time, he spent a ton of money we didn't have to travel to a convention in Miami with the solitary goal of putting his DVD in the hands of a Black playwright named Je'Caryous Johnson. We're talking plane tickets, a hotel room, and entrance to a five-hundred-dollar-per-plate gala. The idea was to approach Mr. Johnson, shake his hand, and give him the DVD, upon which Mr. Johnson would immediately watch the DVD, sign Kev, and take him right out on tour. Instead, Je'Caryous walked out of the gala, accepted the DVD, and kept walking. Kev returned home with nothing but credit card debt. Melissa, the realist, tried to be supportive. But the whole time, she was thinking, *This is dumb and you're dumb.* She knew Kev's dream was just that: a dream, supported by no plan and no money.

The two of us are different in so many respects, from our attire (can you guess who is all about the sweatpants and who prefers to get dressed up?) to our work and sleep schedules. If one of us is up, the other is down; if one goes left, the other goes right. Luckily, we don't think intrinsic personalities and natural compatibility dictate the success of a relationship. Your commitment to the relationship and your willingness to work hard are what determine whether your marriage succeeds or fails.

Marriage be hard. Keeping the fire alive be hard. Reconciling what you've been taught while heating things up in the bedroom takes practice, skill, creativity, and intentional relearning. Ironically, we are doing more work on our marriage now, in year eighteen, than we did when we started out.

Early on, we didn't deliberately put in the work. We were just being married, figuring if we picked the right spouse, read *The Five Love Languages,* and went to church, everything would work out fine. But now we do self-work, individual therapy, and couples therapy. We read books, listen to podcasts, and have tough conversations together. We've learned to connect the dots from childhood trauma to an argument we had in 2003 and all the way up to our life together today. We've faced new seasons and life changes that brought on resentment, jealousy, and communication breakdowns. We've learned a lot—by making mistakes and also by reading and researching the things that make a marriage succeed. That's how you end up happily married for life: You gotta put in the real work.

Doing all that while navigating parenting and social media and whose turn it is to unload the dishwasher? It's freaking hard! Truth is, real marriage is not automatic. It ain't no Tesla on the open road. It's a stick shift on a hill in the rain with no windshield wipers. You're going to have to do some doggone work. Our goal is to make it a little bit easier for you than it was for us, because we're going to be straight up with y'all in a way no one was with us. You just might have a laugh or two as well.

Kevin:

In these pages, we go beyond the rules preached on Sunday mornings and the advice you got from marriage ministries, from men's and women's groups, and certainly from your parents. We're here to give you straightforward advice about how to approach, follow, and maybe even appreciate those rules.

Melissa and I grew up with churchy people holding up the paradigm of how we were supposed to live our lives. We strive to be like Jesus: perfect. But often we've felt more like Paul, with a thorn in our side that never goes away.[2] Carrying that heavy weight is isolating and shame inducing. It can make you feel like you are the only one breaking the rules, like you don't belong. You belong. You are normal. You deserve someone to be honest with you.

We're just the right amount of candid, real, and reckless (responsibly reckless, of course) to be helpful to you, because there's a lot you need to know for the health and well-being of your relationship, both in and out of the bedroom. We're also honest about our own marriage. You're going to hear about the time Melissa kicked me out of her car, about the months early in our marriage when I bordered on the brink of an emotional affair, about the day when I almost beat up one of Melissa's colleagues, and about conflicts we're still working through to this day. I don't kid.

As you read, keep in mind that we are not licensed marriage counselors or experts with fancy letters after our names. (Please don't sue us!) And we're definitely not people with a perfect marriage. We are flawed. We make mistakes all the time, but we learn from them, and our marriage gets better as a result of that learning. In fact, we've come to a ton of revelations even in the process of writing this book. We are two people offering the tips and tricks we've learned over the course of twenty-plus years of dating and marriage, in hopes of making the ride a little smoother for others. We want to pave the road for you that was nothing but gravel and dirt for us.

Melissa:

In this book, you will not only learn about important topics you and your partner should be discussing on a regular basis, but you'll learn *how* to have those conversations. Even the hard ones you've been avoiding for years. Once you talk about these things and get used to checking in with each other about the dynamics that make or break relationships, we think you and your partner will discover how revolutionary it is. Actively discussing important topics with honesty can be transformative for your relationship. It certainly has been for us. This is the manual we wish existed after we said "I do."

Marriage Be Hard

Chapter One

Expectations Be Hard

When you grow up in the church, marriage is set up for you as a fairy tale, a promise that if you follow the rules, you'll get everything you ever wanted and more. But sometimes that promise doesn't deliver. We had those expectations, but when we got to the reality of what marriage is—the reality we didn't see at the end of movies, when the prince and princess ride off on beautifully groomed horses—we weren't prepared for much of what we found.

Kevin:

I'll never forget the first time I saw Melissa. It felt like the beginning of a fairy tale; I'm not gonna lie. It was August 1999, the first day of eleventh grade, and I walked into Ms. Chapman's U.S. history class. There was Melissa, sitting in the fourth row, and she was the most beautiful person in the classroom. Not only was she gorgeous, but she was talking to three or four other people and commanding the conversation. Everyone looked gripped by whatever she was saying. I took a seat in the fourth row, as close to her as possible, and sat there thinking about how to approach her.

All of a sudden, I received a tap on my shoulder. The young gentleman behind me, in his braids and glasses, handed me a note and asked me to pass it to the girl two seats over. I thought, *Oh no, he likes her too.* But she gave the folded piece of paper a cursory glance and put it down without reading it. I took that to mean I had a chance. That guy was going to be no competition.

Melissa:

I could tell you about the girl in our chemistry class that Kevin liked. Or the other girl at our church that he had his eye on. Or so many other girls. In fact, I used to call him the Fisherman because he would just cast out his line and whichever girl bit, he would date her. It was Madison; then it was Abigail; then it was Hannah. He was a player, and that was not for me.

Kevin:

I had someone in each of Melissa's classes campaigning for me to get her to date me. It didn't work until May of our junior year, when Tony (my friend and Melissa's cousin) practically begged her to go out with me. "Come on, cuz. Give my boy Kev a chance." She was so annoyed, she grabbed my hand and said, "Fine, Tony. I will date him. Are you happy now?" And then she threw my hand away from her.

Melissa was the worst girlfriend I ever had. The absolute worst. Of all the girls I dated, she cared the least about me. She didn't want to hold my hand. She didn't want to hug or kiss me. She acted like she didn't care if we were together or not. My previous girlfriends wrote me notes. They fried up chicken for me and brought it to my basketball practices. I used to tickle my girlfriends on their knees (it was sort of my move), but when I tried it with Melissa, she asked me what I was doing and told me never to do it again. Melissa didn't even care if I walked her home from the bus. She was cold as ice. She sucked as a girlfriend. But I loved her so much, I didn't care that she sucked.

After junior year, I went to El Paso for the summer to see my grandma, and Melissa and I did the long-distance thing. This was before I had a cellphone, and there was no way my grandma was going to let me run up her long-distance bill. Melissa and I wrote real letters back and forth, but we didn't see each other all summer. Something changed over those months. On the first day of twelfth grade, I walked home with a friend of mine. Melissa was mad, talking about "I haven't seen you all summer and you don't even want to walk me home?" I was like, "You have never cared about anything I have done or said. Ever." It was then that I realized she actually liked me. Four months after we started dating.

In the spring of our senior year, we went on a youth church retreat to Ocean Shores, Washington, which is the ugliest beach ever. When you picture a beach, you might imagine white sand, clear blue water, and a gentle breeze blowing in your hair. Ocean Shores was the opposite: all rocks, muddy water, and cold, harsh wind. We were sitting together on the church van and Fred Hammond's "Thank You Lord" was playing. I was overcome with emotion, and I said to Melissa, "I'm thankful to Jesus for you, and I love you." To my great surprise, she said it back.

Melissa:

I was not *playing* hard to get. I actually *was* hard to get. I finally warmed up in twelfth grade. I realized I was being stubborn and difficult for no reason. I asked myself, *What more does this guy have to prove?* He was a good person, and I knew that. We dated through senior year; then Kev followed me to college at the University of Washington.

On Easter Sunday 2003, our sophomore year, we were all in church. Kev got up in front of the packed pews and started talking about how important God's sacrifice was and that the church was the bride of Christ. I wasn't sure of his point, but there was something about how the ring is a symbol of a union like the cross is the symbol of the Lord. He was going on and on about the commitment to love and God's commitment to us. Then he asked me to go up and stand with him in front of the 112 people packed into that church. Next thing I knew, my two sisters and two friends walked in, each holding a poster board. One by one, they turned their poster board around, revealing a word at a time: *Will. You. Marry. Me.* And the *Me* sign had a drawing of two rings.

I had no idea it was coming. In fact, the day before Easter, I went shopping with my mom and our church's first lady, and they were pushing me to buy a new outfit for Easter. I was like, "First of all, it's Easter. Why are we worried about a new outfit? That's the problem with the world today. Too many people think Easter is about the outfit. I don't really care."

I'm actually angry that they didn't force me to buy something that day or at least make me choose something prettier out of my closet. I ended up wearing a long-sleeved tunic with an attached cape. It was so bad. I looked like a pilgrim. When Kevin called me up in front of everyone, it still didn't occur to me that he was going to propose. Not until the card *Marry* was flipped over did I realize what has happening. I was shocked. He got down on his knee and gave me the ninety-nine-dollar ring that we had picked out together at the military post exchange. (Yes, I had helped pick out the ring, and I still didn't know that he was proposing.)

It goes without saying that I said yes. Kevin had all the things I knew were important in a husband—the list many of us make in our heads when we're picturing our lifelong partner. Now listen, I'm not talking about superficial stuff like "tall, dark, and handsome." I didn't care about Kevin's career path or family money. I'm talking about the morals, values, and character that make men who they are. Even at twenty years old, I knew that those were the nonnegotiables that carry a relationship in conflict and hard times.

Here are the nonnegotiables we had back when we were first starting out:

Melissa's Nonnegotiables	Kevin's Nonnegotiables
Christian	Christian
Respect for family	Got along with my family
Good grades	Would make a good mother

Obviously, each of us determined that the other had all the vital attributes that made for a perfect life partner, so we agreed to take the vows. We got married on June 26, 2004, at a church on Martin Luther King Jr. Way in Tacoma, Washington. For reference, anything that was on K Street or MLK Jr. Way was in the hood. I had a moment alone in the limo before entering the church. I looked out the window at the beautiful day (sunny days are rare in Tacoma, even in June), and I saw all these people walking in and thought, *Oh my God, all these people are here for me and I'm about to get married.* I was nervous and scared about entering this lifelong commitment, but seeing all these people from my family, from high school, from college, and from my church filled me with an overwhelming sense of love and support.

For us kids who grew up saved, marriage is a whole lot different than dating. When you're dating, you basically spend all your time trying not to have sex. Kevin and I were always taking care to put ourselves in safe situations. By that, I mean getting home before it gets too late or not seeing racy movies while sitting close to each other. For us and for other couples who grew up churchy, those were the rules. Then, once you tie the knot, all these new experiences are thrown at you. Being married was the first time we lived together and made real financial decisions. Truth be told, it was the first time I ever paid my own bills. And of course, marriage brought on the biggest change for me: sex.

When you grow up churchy and then get married, you transition from no sex to sex, and that transition happens abruptly, on your wedding night. Kevin and I have never discussed our wedding night publicly, and we think it's important to document the event that took us from one end of the sexual tunnel to the other. A lot of people who grow up saved expect their wedding night to be magical, with fireworks and rainbows and unicorns. But for most people, it ain't like that—and sex isn't the only realm where your expectations for marriage can complicate the real thing. It's kinda like getting excited for your first trip to Disneyland and getting there to find that the parking lot is dirty.

Kevin:

We were juniors in college and had no money. And when I say *no money,* I mean it. We had a total of $384 to spend on our three-day honeymoon in San Francisco, so there was no way we were going to blow a chunk of that on a hotel in Tacoma after the wedding.

Melissa:

Since we were leaving for San Francisco the very next day, we spent our wedding night at Kevin's apartment, which we called the Dungeon because it was belowground. The good news was that the bedroom had a window. The bad news was that it looked up a dirt path that led to a parking lot. That's how broke we were.

While I wish I could say I had huge expectations for the magic of wedding-night sex, the truth is that my good-girl vision of myself didn't allow me to anticipate sex at all. In my family's church, it was made clear that "boys will be boys." They will try and try again to make something happen, whether at the movies, in the car, in the bleachers, or up against the school lockers. It was a girl's job not to tempt them. The pressure was all on us.

Looking back, it makes me sad that I wasn't more excited. I hate that I didn't allow myself deeper thoughts or even consider how I felt about losing my virginity. I mean, here was the night I was finally allowed to have sex free of condemnation, and I had been conditioned not to even think about it. That kind of curiosity was still against the rules.

The only preparation I allowed myself was purchasing some sexy lingerie. Now, when I say *sexy,* you have to remember where I was on the sexy spectrum. If Frederick's of Hollywood was on one end, my white nightgown from Sears would have been at the opposite. I'll tell you this, though: That gown had spaghetti straps. Boy, was I excited about those spaghetti straps! Up until that point, showing shoulders was a big no-no. My parents made it clear that in the pursuit of modesty, there were to be no tank tops, no spaghetti straps, no showing my body. Therefore, my only criterion for my wedding-night lingerie was that my shoulders be bare. But was the gown sexy by the standards I have now? No, not even close. I went into that night with my new nightie, thinking it was all going to be easy and natural. I mean, why wouldn't it be? I had followed the rules and done everything right, so that's how it's supposed to be.

Kevin:

Let me tell you about my apartment, the Dungeon. Thinking about that place now, I recognize that it was terrible, but at the time, it was nice by comparison because a lot of people I knew lived in far worse places. My apartment was five minutes from the mall, and it had a covered, assigned parking spot. I had friends who lived in an area of Washington called Chocolate City, which was the hood, an endless stream of loud music and gunshots. I felt pretty great about myself, having my own place near the mall and specifically not in Chocolate City.

I had an old couch that I had found on the side of the road. The orangey-brown pineapple fabric made it look like something you might see in a photo of your mom sitting in her family's 1970s living room. I thought it was comfortable, but Melissa let me know it was just worn, so what I thought was comfort was really the feeling of sinking into the sagging cushions.

Pots and pans and dishes were expensive, so I ate off paper plates with plastic forks. I had one big spaghetti pot and one small saucepot for ramen noodles. And, of course, a George Foreman grill. No blender, no toaster, no real cups, and a drawer full of condiments from Carl's Jr. and Starbucks. There was no dining room, so I ate every meal and every snack while sitting on that pineapple sofa.

I don't really know what I expected to happen on our wedding night, but I do remember not expecting to have sex. At our wedding reception, a lady from our church who was close to my family pulled me aside and said in my ear, "Don't you try nothin' with Melissa tonight. She's had a long week. She's gonna be tired, and her feet are gonna hurt. Y'all are going on a honeymoon. You can try something tomorrow night. Be respectful of her."

I remember being like, *Well, dang, I've already been waiting for this for like four years. I kinda, like, really wanna do some P in Va-G tonight. But if I held out this long, I can hold out one more night, especially if I am gonna come across insensitive.*

But much to my surprise, Melissa was the one who initiated sex. I was shocked when Melissa came out of the bathroom in that Sears nightgown. I had never seen her in anything sexy. I mean, shoulders? Shoulders! For her, it was a lot! So here I was with zero expectations, and then to my very pleasant surprise, we had sex on our wedding night. Just once, but once was more than I had had in mind, so it was a gift.

And then on our three-night honeymoon in San Francisco, we did it a whole bunch more. I was beyond ecstatic. I was like,

Well, that was fantastic. I got me a little horny kitten. This is gonna be great! My wife was a sexual being, and I was the beneficiary of it. *This is great,* I thought. *This is what it's going to be like forever.*

Melissa:

I'm going back to the analogy of Disneyland here. I remember taking our two boys to Disneyland when we first moved to Los Angeles. At thirty years old, I was probably more excited than the kids. All my life, I had heard of this magical place I couldn't wait to experience. That's how sex was to me: Now that it was no longer forbidden, I was excited, I was nervous, and I was ready!

Yes, I did initiate sex. But I had no idea what I was doing. No one gave me any advice—not my mom, not my friends, no one. I never even asked. Asking about sex conveyed a desire to actually have sex, so I knew not to ask.

When I was growing up, one of the worst things you could be called was a Jezebel. Jezebel was the bad girl of the Bible: manipulative, seductive, and wicked. The word *fast* was thrown around a lot when people gossiped about the girls who tempted boys—even involuntarily. I know a woman, a pastor's wife, who is a full-figured girl. When she started filling out as a teenager, a church woman walked up to her and said, "Ooh, you're getting thick. That probably means you're having sex." It made absolutely zero sense, but if you grew up in that world, you still wanted to avoid being singled out like that. Those were the reasons I never asked for advice about sex, even wedding-night sex.

After the wedding reception, I was at my parents' house along with a whole bunch of family and friends from out of town. Everyone was trying to get me to stay, but I remember thinking, *I gotta go. I got business to take care of.* In the car, on the way from the reception to Kevin's apartment, I had no idea what it was going to feel like. Was I going to enjoy it? Was it going to hurt? I worried that I was going to bleed on his sheets and that would be really embarrassing. But in addition to the fear of the unknown, there was also excitement because I had waited my whole life for this moment. I had reached the good-girl Mount Rushmore. I had waited all this time, and I was now legally married; I had said my vows. It was like getting a sticker that said *You did it!*

After twenty-one years of buildup, I remember thinking that an overwhelming change would come over me once I finally had sex—as if the sexual person that had always been deep inside would come charging through. I had gone to college, earned my degree, and gotten married, and now I was going to emerge from this magical experience a new woman, the sexy version of myself.

Nothing like that happened. After my wedding night, I felt exactly the same as I always had. I looked exactly the same in the mirror as I did before it all. It goes back to the promise: I waited, I didn't have sex, I didn't think about sex, and I did as I was told. Where was the magic?

The other piece of information that would have been useful is that sex is messy, it's awkward, and you're just not good at it right away. When you hear about sex in movies, in books, or from people talking, you're not hearing about first-time sex. You're hearing about good sex, practiced sex. In fact, those stories are usually about the best sex people have ever had. When I lost my virginity, I compared that experience to people's best version of sex, and it did not compare.

To be clear, it was less about the experience itself and more about how I expected the experience to impact me. I had identified myself as a Christian. I was part of the purity movement; I had saved myself; I was not fast. I was a good girl, so the act of sex should have unraveled all of that. It should have set me free from all those constraints. I didn't have to be a good girl anymore. I did it right. But I was still me, and all the restrictions and restraints were still there. I had to put in the work to shed them.

I think Katt Williams's joke about getting shot is a perfect metaphor for what wedding-night expectations are like for a virgin. Katt says, "I know 50 done made it cool to get shot, ain't nothing cool about gettin' shot. I've been shot before, ain't s**t cool about it. When I got shot, ain't no Music play, ain't no B*****s come out, Nothin'!"[1] By centering my Christianity, my purity, and my identity on whether or not I had done that one act, I put too much pressure on the first time. And that pressure carried over into the first years of our marriage.

Kevin:

I wasn't a virgin, so I didn't feel nervous about the actual act of having sex. But that doesn't mean I wasn't terrified. It was Melissa's first time. I wanted it to be magical for her, and I felt 100 percent responsible for her experience. I was no expert, but I'd had sex and had long been into sexual things. I watched porn; I masturbated; I read *Maxim* magazine. *Cosmo*'s racy stories did the job, and you might be surprised, but the occasional *Good Housekeeping* issue delivered in that department too.

The messages I got around sex were completely different from what Melissa experienced. It was important to me to *not* be a virgin when I got married. I went to church, but I was also in the regular world where every guy I knew was out there having sex or trying to have sex. The summer of 1999 was a wild one for me, back when "Cash Money Records taking over for the '99 and the 2000."[2] There was unspoken peer pressure; you were a dork if you were a virgin. At fifteen, I thought, *I'm going to be sixteen and I'm still a virgin?* I was actively trying to have sex, and there was a huge sense of relief when I finally did it. I was cool. I no longer had to lie when someone asked if I'd had sex. I was a man!

On our wedding night, I went from nervous to excited to relieved. After it happened, I thought, *This is what it feels like to have sex with someone you love. This is what guilt-free, no-condemnation, "I don't care if she gets pregnant; I would be ecstatic to have kids with her" sex feels like.* It was cage-free, organic, non-GMO, no MSG, Whole Foods sex. Every time I had done it before, I would go to church the next day convinced that the pastor knew about it. If the rapture happened before I had time to repent, I would be left on earth with all the other sinners. But that first time with Melissa just felt different. I loved her so much, and we'd been celibate for the four years we were together. There was a sense of pride in that. *This is what it's supposed to feel like!* Afterward, I slept like a baby in a bassinet.

Melissa:

The shame about sex wasn't present on our wedding night or even on our honeymoon. After all, that was vacation sex (which I list as one of my most sensitive accelerators in chapter 3, "Sex Be Hard"). For many people, the honeymoon is their first foray into vacation sex, and in my experience, it kind of set me up for the okey doke. When you return from your honeymoon, you come down from the high, and you are back in real life with work and school and all the adjustments those things entail.

Kevin and I had to get used to each other as roommates, which wasn't as trivial as it sounds. Just becoming accustomed to each other's habits and quirks was an adjustment. Kevin used to put leftover soda from fast-food restaurants in the fridge. I'm talking plastic cups with lids and straws, lined up on my refrigerator shelf, sitting there waiting to get flat. Who does that? Similarly, learning that I had idiosyncrasies that were annoying to him was a revelation: "Who, me?"

Starting your life together is not like riding on the perfect horse to the perfect castle. Quite the opposite actually: It's when the work begins. It's when you figure out how to be married, how to live together, how to make your relationship a priority, how to be vulnerable with each other for optimal communication. From that day forward, you need to be intentional about how you operate as a married couple. You need to be deliberate about getting to the "happily ever after." Not just in the bedroom but everywhere.

Relationship Check-In

Throughout this book, we recommend having regular relationship check-ins with your partner. We find these check-ins to be highly productive for us, and we use them regularly to discuss looming issues as well as annoying little details. You will find them at the end of each chapter, and we suggest you use them to keep the conversations between you and your spouse frequent and deliberate. Here's the assignment for your first relationship check-in:

- What assumptions did you bring into your marriage?
- Has your marriage lived up to your expectations?
- What about your marriage is better and more satisfying than you ever thought possible?

Chapter Two

Communication Be Hard

It goes without saying that communication is required in every relationship, whether it's with your co-workers, your friends, your parents, your children, or—of course—your spouse. Everyone knows that. But what does that really mean? When someone says, "Communication is key," what kind of communication are they talking about? How often are we supposed to communicate effectively? And whose responsibility is it to do all this communicating?

Even though this chapter is dedicated to communication, the subject is sprinkled throughout the book because communication affects all aspects of a relationship—from sex to fighting to jealousy and so on. We want your communication to be firing on all cylinders. As you'll read, we think communication is most effective when you and your partner are able to express yourselves and be heard and understood. Likewise, the reaction you get from your partner after expressing yourself effectively should be free of judgment, ridicule, and aggression.

The problem is, a lot of us do a terrible job of actually communicating. When our partners do something that hurts us, instead of us explaining why we're hurt and what we'd like to have happen differently the next time, our feelings propel us to hurt back. We respond with something sarcastic or below the belt or a holdover from a previous disagreement, and we end up having an argument about something vastly different from what we were trying to communicate.

When we moved to Los Angeles in 2013, we had two cars: a 2009 Toyota Corolla, which Melissa drove, and a 1996 Honda Civic, which Kev drove until the transmission broke. Kevin, without communicating with Melissa, thought it was a foregone conclusion that a new car was in order. After all, the Civic's transmission was trash, it would cost $3,000 to fix, he had to get to work, and renting a car would be more expensive. So he went and bought a new Honda Accord for Melissa, with a low $279 monthly payment and no money down. He felt like a total hero, thinking he went out and did the manly thing. Melissa, the only one in the household with a regular paycheck, did not find that heroic at all. Buying a new car was a big purchase that, in her mind, should be discussed as a couple. It was a big problem—like a someone-has-cheated kind of problem. The communication *about* buying the car was nonexistent, and thus the communication *after* having bought the car was tense and ineffective.

We have learned that there is no such thing as a foregone conclusion in a marriage. What you think is obvious might not be obvious to your partner. Even if it is obvious, it warrants a conversation and an agreement. Safe to say, we have learned a lot since then.

For this chapter, we're going to define *effective communication* as "the ability to be honest, transparent, and vulnerable in delivering your message to your partner." And it involves much more than simply talking. News flash: For us, it took a lot of trial and error to get it right, and sometimes we still fail. We're here to tell y'all, though, it makes a huge difference in your relationship when you communicate effectively.

Melissa:

I'm going to start talking about effective communication with a story where I did *everything* wrong! You hear me? Everything!

Okay, here goes:

In 2014, around the same time that Kevin was rising in social media popularity, I was working for a small aerospace company. When I started, I didn't get too close to my co-workers, pretty much subscribing to the philosophy of "Y'all know me from nine to five, but when I clock out, we no longer know each other until I clock in again at nine a.m." (Side note: I was the only Black woman in the office.) Was this the smartest, most congenial approach for building my corporate career? Probably not. But I'm sure I'm not the only one who doesn't mix business with pleasure.

Even though I tried to keep my private life private, I did warm up to my colleagues, particularly when my husband's comedy started showing up in people's Facebook feeds. Often I would walk into the office after one of Kev's videos went viral, and my co-workers would ask, "Are you married to KevOnStage?" I was a little embarrassed because I don't like attention, but a small part of me was also proud. (Fun fact: The last part of that sentence is a perfect example of effective communication, because I'm being honest, transparent, and vulnerable in admitting that I took pride in the fact that my husband's hard work had paid off and his name, as well as mine, was known. But keep reading. We'll get to that later.)

After working at the job for several years and growing to

genuinely like my colleagues, I started accepting invitations to hang out with them after work. Since Kevin worked in the evenings, he was usually too busy to join us—and when he was legit unavailable, I completely understood his not being there. But there were three occasions in particular when Kevin could have attended and I really wanted him to, but he declined. One time, Kev said he'd attend a company holiday party with me, so I told my colleagues he'd be there. When he changed his mind and I had to face several versions of "I thought Kevin was coming," . . . Chile, I snapped.

This is an opportunity to expand on a dynamic that I believe exists between many couples. Often, instead of admitting that our feelings are hurt or that we feel rejected, our first reaction is to get angry. My work holiday party was on the calendar a month in advance, and Kevin agreed to join me. Then, at the last minute, Kevin's company threw their party together and planned it for the same night. I said, "Really? Seriously? You told me you were coming, and I told my co-workers you were coming. That sucks. What am I supposed to do?" Kevin had no answer for me. So, you know what I did? I said "Fine" and stormed out. It was like a game of Jenga. Every time you pull out a piece of the structure, you create a hole in the foundation, and eventually the whole thing comes tumbling down.

Before I go into how I completely failed on the communication front, I need to provide a little more context. At the time, Kevin was working in digital media for a cool company with cool people. To give you an idea how his work life compared to mine, think back to high school. Remember how the cool kids always sat together at lunch? The beautiful, talented, athletic ones? That was Kev's workplace environment—the cool kids' table—while mine was the table of dorks and misfits. I don't mean that disrespectfully, because I genuinely grew to love my co-workers, but we definitely were not sitting with the prom queen and high school quarterback. Kevin had his dream job where he got to create and play, meet celebrities, and post on social media. And as if that wasn't enough, he and his co-workers would have footraces in the parking lot and film them. Have I made myself clear about the cool factor? I think so. My friend group at work included a random collection of people: twenty-three-year-old college students, sixty-year-old grand-fathers, middle-aged men and women. We easily could have been on a poster for diversity and inclusion.

Still, the imbalance got under my skin. When it came down to it, I always went with Kev to his work events, attending plenty of parties where I stood in a corner while Kev mixed and mingled. Very often, all I wanted to do was scream and go home. Socially, I was the epitome of the Alessia Cara song "Here." ("Truly I ain't got no business here . . . I would rather be at home all by myself."[1]) And that was fine. I had been by Kev's side for countless outings, gatherings, dinners, luncheons— you name it—recognizing that his events meant more for his career. I got it. But to me, this was less about career importance and more about how we supported each other and each spent time on things that were important to the other.

Let me tell you, it was plainly obvious to me that my feelings didn't matter to Kev. At all. When Kev was invited to my com-pany events, whether they were small get-togethers or larger corporate parties, I very often RSVP'd no for him without even discussing it. But that hadn't been the case for this holiday party. It was the one thing I absolutely wanted to attend with my husband.

At the last minute, Kevin told me he wasn't coming be-cause something else came up. Normally, I'm not a person who keeps score, but when I tell you I'd had enough, . . . I was done! I simmered on that until a few weeks later, when Kev and I got ready to attend his co-worker's wedding. Kevin's brother and his wife were at our house, and we were all dressed up and excited about dancing and partying at the reception. But when it was time to leave, I said, "I'm not going because I'm too tired." Kevin looked at me with a mix of confusion and shock. I thought I was finally showing him how he made me feel all these years.

The problem is that my communication was not effective. Not even close. As you can imagine, Kevin and my sister- and brother-in-law were very surprised. "How in the world did we go from laughing, joking, and having a good time to *this*?" Their genuine surprise is what let me know that I didn't effectively communicate.

Communication is a team sport in which all players are required to read from the same handbook. When I changed my attitude without warning, I essentially switched up the play without informing my teammates. And to compound the situation, when they asked what was wrong, I didn't tell them where my feelings originated. So now they were left completely in the dark.

Kevin had no idea I was hurt from the times he'd skipped my work events. I never said anything, so why in the world would he know the reason behind my boycotting this wedding? Did I really think that Kev was going to ponder it and think, *Hmm, I wonder why she's not coming. She says she's tired, but maybe I've done something wrong somewhere. Perhaps Melissa is perturbed that I have not gone with her to her work parties. I have learned my lesson!* No! That did not happen. He took my words at face value, which makes perfect sense.

Everyone left the house for the wedding, while I stayed home, stewing in my own juices. Now, I do enjoy my alone time every now and again, but this was just plain dumb. Kevin had no idea that I had chosen to die on that hill. In fact, he didn't even know there *was* a hill. I had not effectively communicated any of the feelings or thoughts behind my choice.

Years later, after Kevin and I had started therapy and realized how bad we were at communication, I came up with three pillars—a trifecta of sorts—for effective communication. Of the three, *honesty* comes first. You're not going to get anywhere meaningful with your spouse unless you're honest. I failed on that front in this scenario. When I refused to go to the wedding, I said it was because I was tired. That wasn't honest, not even close. And that's the thing: While I do believe that most people make every effort to be honest in their relationships, the fact is that we often fail.

My lack of honesty with Kevin did not arise because I intended to be devious. It happened because I hadn't gone through my process of (1) thinking through my feelings, (2) being honest with myself in determining whether I was on the right side of the issue, and (3) bringing that honesty to Kevin. Honest communication is the fastest way to mutual understanding, and the fact of the matter is that I concealed my true feelings about the issue for a long time. If I had been honest about how all those missed events made me feel, Kevin and I would have been reading from the same playbook, allowing us to work through the issue faster and keep resentment from building up.

Now, it's also true that you can use the excuse "I'm just being honest" to say something that stings your partner. For example, I might have told Kev that I wasn't going because I wanted to get back at him. That would have been honest, but it would also have been spiteful, mean, and childish. Honesty should be paired with kindness. Because, well . . . why not? You can be honest and still not be communicating effectively. Which brings me to the next component of effective communication: *transparency.*

Transparency means taking honesty to the next level. It requires being accountable to your motivations—your true motivations—and identifying them in the first place. If honesty is the *what*, transparency is the *why*. Transparency is identifying the reason behind the feelings, the behavior, or the communication breakdown.

Here's a hypothetical example of the need for transparency. If a husband gets a talking-to at work and is at risk of being demoted, receiving a pay cut, or even getting fired, he might feel emasculated and not be honest with his wife about what happened. His insecurity might manifest itself in his behavior, making him moody, cranky, or short-tempered. If he's being transparent with his wife, he will admit that he's afraid she's going to view him as less of a man. He will admit that his work problems threaten his masculinity, his role as a provider. Communicating with transparency builds trust and fortifies honesty. The conversation is no longer just about telling my truth; it's also about understanding why I'm acting and responding the way I am.

You can't have transparency without a foundation of honesty. In the story above, if I had been transparent, I would have explained that I had been hurt by Kevin and I wanted him to understand what it felt like to walk into a work event alone when everyone else had their partners there. I might have said that it was his turn to have to answer to his friends and colleagues when they asked, "Where is Melissa?" And while it certainly would have sent a message, that still wouldn't have been effective.

Maybe you've had an outburst or two and said something

similar in anger to your partner. And the thing is, you can rest knowing you were honest and transparent! (Insert Tyrese meme here: "What more do you want from me?" I know! I know!) But the hard work is what comes next: *vulnerability*.

Being vulnerable means exposing yourself to rejection. You admit that you're jealous, that you're afraid of losing your partner, that you're insecure. Vulnerability invites your partner to the deepest, darkest, even ugliest parts of you. If transparency allows you to recognize the issue, vulnerability allows you to share it.

It's a natural human instinct to avoid vulnerability, avoid being exposed, and thus avoid putting yourself in harm's way. That's why people tend to do anything and everything to keep from speaking vulnerably. And when I say "*people*," I mean me. Vulnerability is scary, because when you're vulnerable, you risk getting hurt. But you have to be vulnerable with your partner in a way you don't have to be with others. Your spouse needs to understand you to support you in the way you need, to know you better than anybody else does.

If I wanted Kevin to fully understand my position, I should have added vulnerability to my statement. Let's break it down:

- **What I felt:** I felt rejected. I felt that what mattered to me didn't matter to my husband. I felt embarrassed that I had to explain to my colleagues time and again why my husband wasn't present. I was hurt that Kevin didn't consider my feelings and didn't place value on the parts of my life that didn't include him. He was not attending any of my work parties, and to get him back, I did the exact same!
- **What I actually said:** "I'm not going to the wedding because I'm tired." No honesty there.

- **What I might have said if I were simply honest:** "I'm not attending your co-worker's wedding because you never attend things that are important to me!" While that's honest, it's definitely not effective.
- **What I would have said if I were honest and transparent:** "I'm not attending your work event because you never attend mine and I want you to feel the same sadness and shame that I feel when I walk into an event and everyone else has their spouse on their arm and you're never with me. It's your turn!"
- **What I would have said if I were honest, transparent, and vulnerable:** "I'm not attending your work event because I'm angry and hurt. You don't seem to value my work the way I value yours. Also, I have been wanting to show you off to my colleagues, and I feel like a fool when I show up without you. It means a lot to me that you show up in ways that are important to me, even if they aren't important to you."

Kevin:

Here's the crazy thing about Melissa's story. This whole thing was happening for her, in her head and in her heart, and I was in the dark. I had no idea she felt that way about the imbalance in how we supported each other. No idea at all. Quite honestly, it was only while writing this book with her that I became aware that I don't check in often enough about her feelings.

You're probably thinking, *How on earth could Kevin not know that Melissa didn't like attending his work events?* Well, it's twofold: First, I told myself she was having a good time; and second, I was not recognizing the inequality between us, the very thing that was silently fueling Melissa's anger. Obviously, I knew she wasn't having the time of her life when she came out with me, but I didn't really grasp that she was coming to those events for me, not for her own enjoyment. She adopted the *Madagascar* penguins' approach: "Just smile and wave, boys. Smile and wave."[2] And you know what? It worked! Whenever we arrived at a party or gathering, Melissa was always smiling. Always pleasant. She warmly greeted the people she already knew and was friendly to the new people she met. After the initial hellos, she usually chilled and made the requisite amount of small talk while I gallivanted and frolicked through the event being the dapper charmer that I am known to be. My ego was so big, I assumed, *Of course she wants to be at 1 Oak.* (If you're not familiar with it, 1 Oak is a big, fancy club where rappers and other rich, fashionable people gather. Forgive the braggy name-dropping, but I have to tell you that my company had a party there. Rihanna was in attendance, and Justin Bieber performed—after we were home and already asleep, but who cares?)

The truth is, I was so happy going to these clubs and parties, I never took the time to consider whether Melissa loved them as much as I did. But I should've. I know Melissa. She don't care about no nightclub rappers' shout-out. If I took even one second to see past what I wanted to be true, I would have known she was *only* being a dutiful wife.

One thing that I hate about myself is this: I have often been completely unaware of Melissa's feelings. Especially early in our marriage. Actually, it was Melissa who made me aware of this shortcoming. A couple of years ago (years after these work events took place), Melissa pointed out to me that she constantly reads my body language so she can tell if something she says or does makes me feel a certain kind of way. If she sees that her words or actions don't land well, she adjusts accordingly so as to not hurt my feelings. It was only after she described this habit that I realized I didn't tune in to her on that level at all. When I said something to Melissa, I didn't look to see if she smiled or winced. I noticed only if she had a *big* reaction. I had to be hit over the head. If she reacted subtly or passively, I missed it. I said what I had to say and moved on without getting any feedback.

Still, Melissa can be crying real tears, and if I ask her what's wrong, she'll often say, "Nothing." She won't talk about it; she'll just go off to cry in the shower and refuse to tell me what's wrong. And here's where I'll get vulnerable. When this happens, I end up going down a spiral of insecurity in my own head: *My wife is crying, and she won't talk about it. I don't know why she's crying. She's going to hide her tears in the shower; she's going to tell a friend that she's unhappy. She'll meet a man who will understand what she's crying about. She'll leave me for this man, and I will be the one crying in the shower.*

Just as I admit where I fall short, let me also point out where I'm strong. When an issue is brought to my attention, something I need to improve, I work very hard to make the necessary adjustments. I want our marriage to be healthy and happy, and I'll do anything in my power to ensure that. If Melissa had been honest, transparent, and vulnerable back then about how my missing her events made her feel, I would have immediately corrected the problem. Even now, as I type this, I see how in our relationship I haven't been as supportive of Melissa in her endeavors as she has been of me in mine. Of course, I would cheer her on and not obstruct her, but I most definitely didn't show up for her in the ways she did for me.

Now, as her influencer career grows, I can correct where I used to fail. Instead of only *letting* her do her thing, I make it clear that I am there for her in every possible way, both literally and figuratively. For example, when her photo shoots are planned well in advance, instead of just recognizing that she's busy and not asking her to come on the road with me, I could take it to the next level and make sure I don't have a gig that day so I can show up for her. In this phase of our relationship, it's time to even the scales.

I have learned a lot since Melissa blew off that co-worker's wedding. After doing *The Love Hour* and going to therapy, I'm more aware of her feelings and my habit of misreading her cues. I wish we could go back in time and communicate effectively about what was really going on. (But since she didn't speak up and I was unaware of her true feelings, I take zero responsibility for my actions and actively shift the blame to her. I kid. I kid.)

I did learn and I did communicate effectively in a more recent example. Just as we were getting back to life after Covid-19, I started traveling again, and one of the first nights I was back, I thought Melissa and I were going to be home together, watching television. About an hour after I walked in the door, Melissa told me she was going over to her best friend Danni's to hang out. I could have been a big baby and pouted without saying anything, or I could have thrown a temper tantrum. In fact, my natural inclination was to say, "Girl, you always going over to Danni's house. You don't ever make no time for me." But I stopped myself and said, "You know, I've been gone a lot. We made plans to watch TV, and I was really looking forward to that. I've missed you, and I hoped we could have the day together." Because I was honest, transparent, and vulnerable, Melissa heard me, respected my true motivations, and changed her plans to stay home with me.

Melissa:

The truth is, it takes effort to be honest, transparent, and vulnerable. If there's an issue that needs resolving, if there's a breakdown in communication, things will not get solved unless we strive to be effective. In my frustration and anger about our work parties, I did not take the time or make the effort to communicate effectively, and the whole thing blew up in my face. I took a stand in my own head, and Kevin had no clue that I even had a stand to take.

I'm going to add to my definition of effective communication because I think another layer is important: You need to be able to effectively articulate your thoughts, feelings, and emotions in a way that the receiver not only understands but also receives without getting defensive or dismissive. Be careful to choose words that don't make your spouse feel blamed, because then the defense mechanism might kick in. For us, those words are "You always . . ." Any sentence that starts that way leads to trouble. Be mindful of messages that could be taken as finger-pointing. Lead by describing your feelings instead of criticizing your partner's actions.

Our relationship check-ins actually started recently, in quarantine, when my therapist suggested I use an app to write down my feelings about our marriage. Here I was, writing all these complaints down, making a list of things Kev did to bother me, but he didn't know about any of it. It certainly wasn't doing our relationship any good. In fact, it ended up feeling like I was keeping evidence of all the reasons I was angry at my husband. I decided to ditch the app and make it verbal instead. That's how the relationship check-ins were born. It's been a huge step in our effective communication.

Here's an account of one of our recent relationship check-ins:

Last year, Kevin and I were discussing ending the *Love Hour* podcast. We'd had a ton of conversations about it, and despite knowing how to effectively communicate, I hid some of my real reasons for wanting to end the podcast, which included recognizing that the schedule was putting a lot of strain on Kevin's time and energy. He's a traveling comedian with a ton of things to do when he's home, and I wanted to gift him with some of his time back. These were my unsaid sentiments. The podcast was a moneymaker, so walking away from it also meant leaving income on the table, but when I did mention that to Kevin, he encouraged me to not worry about the money. He said we would be fine, which provided me with a lot of peace about walking away.

Fast-forward to after I made the public announcement that we were bringing the podcast to a close. Kevin and I were in the car, and he mentioned that he was going to start a new podcast. I immediately became defensive, and my feelings were hurt. He said one of his primary reasons for starting a new one was that he needed to replace the money we were making from *The Love Hour*. I was offended and a little dejected. Here I was, trying to give him his time back, and he immediately filled it with something else. I sat there stewing, telling myself that he was never interested in hosting with me to begin with. But instead of going down the spiral that I normally do (like I did when I blew off his colleague's wedding), I pivoted and launched a check-in.

I said, "Hey, can we talk about this? Honestly, I'm feeling a little like you never wanted to do the podcast in the first place. And furthermore, the instant you had gained more time to spend with family or relax a bit, you filled it with another item on your to-do list." The conversation was uncomfortable and a little intense, but by the end, Kevin was able to explain some deep fears he'd been carrying about being able to take care of his family. He explained that he would always be willing to bear the burden of maintaining our financial security.

Kevin said he wanted me to be the "queen in the castle." He wanted to protect me at all costs, which meant he was willing to exert himself to exhaustion if that's what it took. I want to be clear: This is noble; this is beautiful. This man clearly loves me and his family. But I don't want to be the queen kept in the castle. I want to be his battle mate. I told Kev that I wanted to be by his side in the fight, swords drawn, facing the enemy together. The lack of clear communication between us made me feel like my contribution wasn't valued and that my husband didn't want to work with me. It was a clear case of bad communication, but the check-in allowed us to work through our feelings, hear each other, understand each other, and end up on the same page.

Kevin:

A lot of times, we fail to effectively communicate for fear of what our partners will think, feel, or say. We think we're protecting their feelings, but theirs end up getting hurt. I have started encouraging Melissa to speak up for herself, because for too many years, I was writing Melissa's responses for her in my head, and those responses were always negative. I realized that in the midst of a conversation, I would be on high alert, bracing for the worst possible response, but when Melissa came out with what she had to say, it completely surprised me. It rarely tracked with what I thought was going to come out. I had been breaking down the lines of communication between us for so long that I didn't even know I was doing it.

You might think that keeping your feelings to yourself is keeping the peace. And maybe it works that way at first. But that thing is going to go unsaid for a long time—weeks, months, years. Eventually, the dam is going to break, and it's all going to spew out. Suddenly instead of just talking about the fact that he doesn't remove his shoes in the house, you're fighting about the fact that he doesn't make the bed or clear the dishes or remember your anniversary and that his job isn't good enough and that's why the two of you are stuck in a small house.

When you don't speak up on your own behalf, resentment builds up. Here's a recent example. When we get in bed, I'm tired, and I know I've got to be at the gym at five a.m. Melissa, on the other hand, can't fall asleep until she watches every episode of *Grey's Anatomy*. Most of the time, my instinct is to not say anything. After all, even though I'm dead to the world, if Melissa is awake in the bed next to me, there's a glimmer of hope that sex might occur. But if given the choice between sleep and watching McDreamy and McSteamy battle it out, I choose sleep. I'd like the television to be off, but I don't want to make Melissa mad. So I end up watching with her, and the next morning at the gym, I'm dragging. If I keep going like this, I'm going to resent her.

If I were to communicate effectively, I would say, "Liss, I'm dog tired, but I'm up for the butt-butt if you are. If not, could we please turn off the TV? Otherwise I'm going to be exhausted tomorrow."

When your partner doesn't communicate, sometimes you can tell something is wrong but you don't know what it is, so you assume the worst. To break this cycle, Melissa and I came up with a solution. Here's how it goes: If I notice that Melissa seems off, I ask her what's up. The agreement we now have is that I will accept whatever answer she gives. So, if she says, "I'm fine" or "Nothing's wrong," I will know that means there's nothing for me to do and I should leave it alone. Melissa knows that if she says she's all good, she has to be accountable to it because I'm going to choose to believe her. But our agreement also gives her agency to speak up when something is bothering her.

The other night, we had friends over for dinner, and the moment they walked out the door, Melissa's energy immediately dropped to near zero. I figured that I had done something wrong. My plan had been to try to have sex after they left, but the way her mood shifted, I knew that was off the table. I asked her if she was okay. She said yes, but I knew she wasn't. So I pushed a little bit. She admitted that she felt insecure. One of the female friends at our house that night had been laughing and joking around with me in a way that, while not flirty or sexual, was a kind of fun Melissa and I don't often have. Melissa's admission was a win. In the past, she wouldn't have revealed why she was upset until much later. But in that moment when we weren't communicating, I knew how to speak to her feelings. She appreciated my effort, and we had a very productive conversation about it, which was an even bigger win.

But sometimes the system breaks down. One time, at the beginning of quarantine, when we were getting used to being home all day and night together, Melissa seemed quieter than usual. I followed the rules, asked her what was wrong, and believed her when she said she was fine. I took her at her word and left the room to watch *The Office* by myself, even though that didn't feel right to me. Sure enough, she was mad. "Oh, so, now you're just going to be away."

Leaving her alone didn't help, but pushing her for an answer didn't help either. I felt helpless. I didn't know how to make her feel safe enough to tell me what she was thinking. I couldn't force her into a good mood. I was at my wit's end. I just distanced myself, hoping it would pass.

Melissa:

Guilty as charged! One of my worst habits is recognizing a problem and then creating the environment for the problem to persist. I have a real fear of being needy or being a nag. So, in my efforts to avoid those labels, I can be guilty of sending mixed messages. I want to feel and act like an independent woman, but secretly I want Kev around more than I care to admit, and I don't know how to articulate it.

This comes up a lot in our marriage. We can be at home watching television, sitting on separate sofas, and instead of saying, "Hey, I want you to come sit next to me," I say, "You just don't ever want to be beside me. Just go then." When he goes, it confirms that my fear is justified and leaves me feeling even more insecure. Or sometimes, when Kevin is on his way home, he'll call and ask me if I'm hungry. When I say no and he comes home with no food for me, my feelings are hurt.

One night I was hanging out at my friend Danni's house, and I texted Kev that I was going to be late so he shouldn't wait up. When I got home at one a.m. and found Kev asleep, I was legit mad that he didn't stay up to make sure I got home safely. Here were the mixed messages:

1. I'm an independent woman, and I can do what I want.
2. You need to be concerned about my well-being. I could have been dead in a ditch!

It's a whole self-fulfilling prophecy resulting from ineffective communication.

Kevin:

Yes, Melissa, my beautiful wife, won't ask for what she needs. She goes so far out of her way to avoid being a nag (which she probably started doing after the first time I called her a nag) that she ends up internalizing all her feelings and keeping the things I do that upset her tucked away inside.

It turns out the behavior we used to refer to as nagging was actually Melissa's making sure she had a voice and that I was listening. It was her speaking up about the things that she didn't like, even if it was just about cleanliness or my sweatpants. My labeling it "nagging" shined a negative light on it and made her want to avoid it at all costs. And it allowed me to weasel out of the things I didn't want to do. What I had essentially done was make Melissa fearful of telling me what bothers her, because she didn't want to feel like, or be called, a nag.

In her defense, though, I'm a crybaby. I can't really handle being told about things I'm doing wrong—especially if it's a bunch of things in a row. I have had to work on taking what she says in stride so she knows she has a soft place to land when she's asking me to make adjustments. I now know what to do when Liss is passive aggressive. For example, in the situation she described above, when we're in the living room together and she wants us to sit closer, I don't need her to say all the words to know what to do: I get my butt up off the chair and go cozy up next to her. That's the thing with being with someone for a long time; you might develop your own way of communicating effectively.

Even though I know what Melissa needs when we're on the sofa in front of the television, things aren't always clear in the bedroom. Over the years, we have had some problems with effective communication when it comes to sex. The truth is, Melissa doesn't turn me down for sex often. But I'm not so good at getting rejected. No one is. It used to be that when she was too tired and didn't want to have sex, I would pitch a fit. I mean, I would turn as far away from her as possible and curl into a ball and pretend to sleep. I was communicating that if she didn't do exactly what I wanted her to do, exactly when I wanted her to do it, then I was going to behave like a spoiled child. She was left feeling that if she said no, I was going to go through the whole rigamarole. Melissa needed agency. She needed me to support her by giving her the opportunity to say yes or no to sex, with no reward or punishment from me either way. When I matured about the whole thing, Melissa felt more valued, allowing her to make the decision that fit her mood and desire instead of worrying how I would react.

The actress and comedian Yvonne Orji once spoke of meeting a fan at an event who asked to take a selfie with her. When she said no to the photo, the fan got upset. She realized that the fan's request wasn't really a question; it was a demand. If you're genuinely asking for something, you should accept and respect the person's yes or no. That's the perfect analogy for our sex life. I had been putting Melissa in the same position, where the only acceptable answer to my request for sex was yes. When I allowed her to voice her own feelings without my throwing a pity party, Melissa felt empowered, and it led to positive changes in our sex life.

We recently had an argument about sex that easily could have been avoided if we had used what we know about effective communication. As you will see when you read the chapter "Sex Be Hard," good smells turn her on and recent pooping turns me off. For us, taking a shower before bed is a path to sex. If one of us asks the other if we'd like to take a shower, that's essentially an invitation to have sex.

One night, we were on track for sex. I mean, things were looking good. But then, I pooped. Again, you will soon read that pooping is an obstacle to sex in our house. There will be no sex unless pooping is immediately followed by a shower. In this instance, I didn't say anything about showering before getting into bed. Melissa, also without saying anything, turned off the light and wrapped herself up in a blanket burrito. The message I got was "I don't want to have sex tonight." But she'd already gotten the same message from me when I pooped and didn't follow up with a shower. As the pooper, I should have said, "Do you want to get in the shower?" But I was mad because I felt like she shut me down by turning off the light. I didn't realize that I'd already sent the first message of rejection.

Both of us could have said something to shift the outcome. This is an example of providing metamessages: relying on nonverbal communication instead of expressing what you really need.

Effective communication takes work. In addition to deciding that the two of you will make an effort, you should pay attention to aspects of your relationship that might be getting in the way. Here are some solutions to roadblocks that inhibit healthy, robust, effective communication.

Using a Soft Start-up

When you want to broach a sensitive subject and you are not looking for an argument, we suggest an intro that clarifies your intention—something like "This is going to be a difficult conversation." Or, "I have something to say that may strike a nerve with you, but I want to have this conversation, and I don't want to upset you." Marriage researcher John Gottman calls this approach the soft start-up. He explains that softening the entry point of an argument is vital to resolving conflicts in your relationship.[3] Coming at your partner with less negativity makes them more receptive to your needs.

If you enter an argument swinging your heaviest ammo, you're going to give the other person emotional whiplash. So, pause at the beginning and frame the conversation. "This has been bothering me for a while, and I want to share it with you to move past it." The soft start-up reminds your partner that you're on the same side and ensures that no one feels attacked.

Kevin:

I think of an easy entry as the very important lubrication to the conversation. In conflict, as in sex, you don't want to just jam it in there. The emotional lube makes talking smoother and easier so the discussion glides without any rough patches.

Another way to keep things silky smooth is the compliment sandwich. Start and finish with something nice. I'm a pro at this. For example, one time, Melissa made chicken meatloaf. Now, to set the stage, traditionally her meatloaf is amazing. She makes it with a mix of ground beef and veal, and the end result is incredible. I mean, better than a greasy-spoon diner's meatloaf. Better than your mama's meatloaf. The type of meatloaf that could beat Bobby Flay. Bobby Flay would come to town with some big-city meatloaf, and the local townspeople would laugh him right out of the city. It is that good.

So, anyway, this one time when she was trying to make us eat healthier as a family, she decided to switch it up and make chicken meatloaf. What a mistake! This meatloaf was God for-saken. This meatloaf wouldn't be fed to soldiers who hadn't had a hot meal in days, for fear of lowering company morale. Nobody in the family liked this meatloaf. Something had to be said.

In that moment, the compliment sandwich looked like this.

Compliment: "Babe, we truly appreciate you making dinner and going out of your way to try and make us healthier as a family. We really, really appreciate that."

Criticism: "However, chickens were never intended to be made into meatloaf. That is not what God wanted out of their lives. It's unnatural. Heaven has turned a blind eye."

Compliment: "Next time, can you go back to the meatloaf you perfected? We love that meatloaf. That meatloaf is amazing. Nothing is wrong with it. The spicy ketchup sauce is the crème de la crème. Thank you again, babe. It's truly appreciated."

Keep in mind that no one likes getting reprimanded. Par-ticularly me. I don't want to hear that I messed up, and I usually try to turn the conversation around by pointing to the things I do well. I take Melissa's critique as an indictment of my entire husbandship and then go looking for examples that disprove what she said. "Remember that time I was a good father?"

One time, Melissa told me I take up too much space in our conversations. I should have closed my mouth and given her plenty of room to talk, but instead I pointed to a time at one of our conferences where I did not take up all the space. And then, being supremely petty and childish, I said, "Fine. You can plan your conference by yourself. I won't help you at all since I take up too much space."

This is how my mind works every time:

What Melissa says: "We don't work together well as a team."

What I hear: "We don't work together well as a team. I don't want to work with you; I don't want to be with you. We're probably getting divorced. There's another guy that I've secretly been talking to that I like, and he'll come home and be my husband."

I know I'm being ridiculous, and these days, I let her know that I know. I now say, "These are my feelings to own and work through." That way, I am being vulnerable, which is something she appreciates. Getting to that point required some self-reflection, self-work, and therapy for me. I had to seek out personal professional help and, later, couples therapy.

There are things I know how to fix. If a joke isn't working in my show, I can make adjustments. But vulnerability is harder, particularly *because* I didn't know it was a thing until I learned that I wasn't good at it. How could I be good at something that I didn't even know I needed to do or have or be? But in a relationship, the stakes are too high to not get it right.

Taking a Break

Melissa:

The next tip for effective communication is actually something Kevin and I don't entirely agree on. It might be a family-oforigin thing. When you're fighting and emotions are running high, I believe in taking a break from the argument and each other. Kev does not. I think a break can provide a chance to cool off and to get some healthy perspective.

Growing up, I saw arguments, but I never saw resolutions. I watched a lot of big feelings erupt with my parents. Their arguments were very unhealthy. I witnessed a lot of yelling and screaming, and after what I thought was taking a break, things seemed better. It was probably just my parents sweeping their issues under the rug, but in my mind, they took a break and recovered from whatever the issue was.

To this day, if Kev and I are having a heated exchange, I get flooded with emotion. I don't know if I want to cry or curse him out, curl up into a ball or punch him. And in general, when a moment gets that tense, I believe you're more likely to forget that you and your partner are on the same side and say something petty just to sting them, which means you'll have to come back and apologize for something you never truly meant. I've found that a soft start-up is far more likely after I've taken a break. Once I have time to process, I can have a clearer conversation.

Kevin:

In my family, we dealt with everything right then and there, so that's what I was used to. My mom and dad argued in front of us in a healthy way. They apologized when they were wrong and took my side when they believed I was right. They would get snippy with each other and then come to a resolution, and that's how I try to approach situations now. But when Melissa and I disagree about something, she often tells me that she doesn't want to keep talking about it. She likes to take a break to avoid things getting worse, so I become a reluctant under-the-rug sweeper.

I do agree that taking a break makes sense if, in the heat of the moment, you're going to say something hurtful and end up arguing about the approach instead of the issue at hand. If you find that you're at an impasse, that you're either not saying anything or saying it at the top of your lungs, it's time to take a break. But sometimes it's hard to reapproach the conversation after you've stepped away because the moment has passed.

Nowadays, when Melissa and I take that needed break, we commit to revisit the situation at an agreed-upon time. Sometimes one of us will say, "Let's both take Jojo to soccer, and during his practice, we can take a walk to discuss this issue." This gives us a specific time and topic, and it keeps the issue from festering. We get the time to decompress, sort out our feelings, let the initial anger subside, and come prepared to work on a resolution.

Work on Non-Ego-First Responses

Melissa:

When you feel like your personhood, not the thing you just did, is being indicted, your internal response might be, *I can't be wrong. Let me defend myself so you can come around to my side.* We're all guilty of responding with our egos first. When your ego gets involved, conflict becomes a scenario where you want to win, and winning often means getting your partner to adopt your opinion.

Instead, try taking your ego out of the equation. Don't ask your partner to explain why they did whatever it was that upset you. Tell them how their behavior made you feel. You want to ensure that you're dealing with the impact. "When you do this, it makes me feel this way."

Kevin:

On one of our early tours, Melissa chose a travel agent who kept making mistakes with our hotels and flights. At one of our stops, I was complaining about the hotel carpet when Melissa's ego jumped in: "If you don't like it, you can book your own hotel." I was like, "I was complaining about the Marriott, not about you." She took it so personally since she had been the one who worked with the travel agent.

After one-too-many complaints, she turned over the job of travel liaison to me, and that's when the tables turned. This year, with a new travel agent and a different tour, people on my team complained about the accommodations. I said, "Y'all can pay for your own rooms from now on if you don't like it." Then I called Melissa and said, "I totally get why you were mad at me." I, too, took it personally. The ego is a fragile thing.

The sting of a badly worded message can pack a huge punch. Whether or not it's your intention, you are responsible for the impact your words and your actions have on your partner. I think a basketball analogy works well here. If you're trying to block a shot in basketball and you hit someone's arm, it's a foul, even if you were going for all ball. You are responsible for the action that happened. In marriage, you're still responsible for the resulting feelings, whether hurting your spouse was your intention or not.

Understand the Difference Between
Accommodation and Compromise

Melissa:

For the purposes of this conversation, compromise is when you and your partner have different wants or needs and you end up meeting in the middle. Both people move off their initial positions, give up something, and reach a new agreement. Accommodation is when one person agrees to the other person's choice. One person fully comes off their position to meet at the partner's desired place. It's essentially giving in.

Both actions are important. But if you're always accommodating, you will ultimately get resentful. To avoid that buildup, you need to be aware when your partner is accommodating and make sure neither of you does it much more than the other.

An example of compromise happened when Kevin and I moved to California back in 2013. At this point in our marriage, we had lived in Washington for thirteen years and were married for nearly ten. We had never seriously discussed moving from Washington. Sure, occasionally we would talk about where we wanted to live *if* we moved. Atlanta for me. Dallas for Kevin. But none of this talk felt real.

At the end of 2012, Isaiah, our older son, had made some comedy videos that went viral and drew the attention of the producers who were rebooting *The Little Rascals*. As big fans of the '90s film, we were excited. Isaiah auditioned and ended up getting picked to play Buckwheat in the new movie. Kevin and Isaiah moved to a small apartment in Los Angeles while the movie shot at Universal Studios.

One fateful day, I got a call from Kevin, and it was obvious his heart was set on moving to L.A. And soon. Yikes! This was a lot for a planner like me. I mean, we were all set in Washington. Good jobs, our own house, kids in private school. Now he wanted to blow this all up for a life of uncertainty in California of all places? I mean, the cost of living alone was terrifying.

At the very least, I wanted to think it over, give it careful consideration, and wait at least twelve months to make a decision. (As you know by now, I like to check my boxes, and these boxes were certainly not checked.) We ended up moving six months later. What makes this a compromise is that both Kevin and I moved from our initial ideas closer to each other's ideal plan. We both gave and we both got. I was glad we were able to save money, pay off debt, and put our house on the market. I didn't get as much time as I would have liked, but I was able to get more than Kev asked for initially, which means he compromised as well.

Accommodations, on the other hand, are one-sided. Back in 2009, Kevin was fired from his job at the bank. I wanted him to hurry up and get another dependable, nine-to-five, paycheck-producing job. I assumed he had the same plan in mind. I was wrong. During a meeting with our pastor, he confessed through tears that he wanted to pursue a career as a stand-up comedian. And I accommodated by supporting his dreams even though it went against my core values.

I believe it's important to acknowledge when your spouse accommodates. Just expressing gratitude for their sacrifice goes a very long way.

Don't get me wrong, I'm not advocating keeping score. It's never going to be exactly equal, but if one person feels that they accommodate far more than their partner does, it's going to lead to resentment and problems. I think the key is that both people can say, "You're showing up for me the same way I show up for you."

Kevin:

Here's how I can tell the difference between compromise and accommodation: It is a compromise if both sides feel a little salty. No one gets everything they want, but no one has to give up everything. Everyone moves an equal amount.

I used to fully believe in keeping score. I grew up playing sports, so the scoreboard was where my bread was buttered. If I went to four of Melissa's events, she needed to come to four of mine. But I have grown up. Now on Monday nights, when my cousin comes over to watch *The Bachelor,* I'm tired but Melissa wants me to stay up and talk with the ladies. I do it and I do it well, offering lots of titillating conversation while I'm practically falling asleep. Melissa knows this is not a compromise; it's something I do not want to do at all. And she appreciates that I accommodate because it's important to her.

I then could go on and say, "I stayed up talking with you and your best friend; therefore, after she leaves, you have to do something for me before we go to sleep." Early in our marriage I would have done that, and it would have erased all the good I did. It would have shown that my heart wasn't in the right place. You have to show up for your spouse without expecting them to repay you in equal amounts. You're not going to get credit every time you accommodate.

To go back to the basketball court for a minute, it's kind of like the possession arrow. In a jump ball, the possessions alternate between teams. If you got what you wanted last time, I get what I want this time. Even though we don't really suggest keeping score like that, in this case, it's like saying, "I recognize and appreciate that you sacrificed for me. The least I can do is sacrifice for you next time."

Relationship Check-In

For the relationship check-in about effective communication, here's what we recommend discussing:

- Is there a specific issue or topic that paralyzes you from communicating effectively with your partner?
- Are there places in your relationship where you have built up resentment?
- What accommodations do you appreciate your partner having made for you?
- What is your biggest stumbling block to being honest, transparent, and vulnerable?

Chapter Three

Sex Be Hard

Here's something you probably didn't know: You can be a Christian and still have a healthy relationship with sex. Revolutionary, right? Yes, it's true, because God is sex positive. Sex was God's idea, and what an idea it was! But if you grew up anywhere near the church, that might not be the message you received. In fact, you might have received the opposite message: Sex is the devil's domain, and thus, sex is anti-God.

As you know, the two of us were raised under heavy influence from the purity movement, which encourages young boys and girls to save themselves for marriage. To be sure, there was some good to this movement, particularly how it told young women that they were worth more than their bodies. Even though that message gets a little lost, the idea that you don't have to give your body away to get a man or keep him is a good one. It's valuable for young women to understand that pressure to have sex is not a characteristic of a healthy relationship. Also, we appreciate the notion that God designed sex for marriage and family, and if done the right way, you can have a beautiful family blessed by God.

The problem is, the message warped into the idea that giving away your virginity, whether you were married or not, meant that you were *not* pure. And if you were not pure (meaning you weren't a virgin on your wedding day), your marriage was effectively doomed. By promoting abstinence at any cost, the purity movement became a breeding ground for shame. Young people internalized shame about their bodies and sex, and we've heard from countless people who felt that shame even after they got married. We don't want to indict the whole church experience, but it definitely had an effect on us.

In the introduction, we made it pretty clear that we were never properly equipped to enjoy a healthy sex life with our spouses. We subscribed to the idea of purity because of the promises it made to us, but since then, we have had to reconcile that much of what we were promised never came to pass. We were told the hard work was doing everything correctly before getting married, but we came to find out that the real work comes later—in our minds and in all the conversations with our spouses that we never even knew we needed to have.

Melissa:

On *The Love Hour,* Dr. Camden Morgante and I discussed how the purity movement made several promises (some actually declared and others implied) to young people, but in this chapter, we're going to focus on three of the biggies.

Promise #1

You Are Significantly More Desirable If You're a Virgin

The best example of this promise—and the subtle yet very present shame it induced—is an anecdote about a piece of chewing gum. One day in Sunday school, when I was around twelve, our pastor held up a piece of gum, brand-new in its perfect foil wrapper. He spoke to all of us, but it was clear that his message was specifically directed at the girls. He pointed out how desirable the piece of gum was. Who would say no when offered a brand-new piece of gum? No one, right? We all agreed, hoping he was actually going to hand out some gum.

He unwrapped it, put it in his mouth, and spent a minute or so giving that piece of gum a good, hearty chew. He then took the wet, chewed-up gum out of his mouth and held it up for all to see. "Who wants this gum now?" Nobody. It was chewed up, full of some other person's saliva. And that, he explained, is what happens to girls after they have sex. (Those weren't the exact words, but they were for sure the subtext.) We would be used, undesirable, and worthy of nothing but the trash can if we were to take our foil wrapper off and succumb to the pressures of sexual activity.

Imagine how that presentation felt to anyone in the room who had already had a sexual experience. And remember, in the purity movement, it's not just sex that makes you impure; it's also sexual thoughts and feelings.

Since then, Kevin and I have met people who had unmarried sex before they found Christianity. When they heard this messaging in church for the first time, they experienced retroactive shame, as if they had been chewed up and spit out. And even though I was a virgin who didn't allow for sexual thoughts, that image—that idea of the shame associated with sex—followed me. For years, my salvation and my relationship with God were solely predicated on the idea of being pure. I held on to that so tightly. My faith in God and my link to godliness was possible only if I stayed a good girl, a virgin. Being pure was what allowed me to have a relationship with Christ, and that relationship could be taken away the moment I slipped up.

Again, these messages weren't just in my head. They were actively reinforced. My first lady once said a prayer over our youth group that if any of us were having sex, God would expose us, meaning through an STD or pregnancy. You wanna talk about a libido killer! Let me tell you, this prayer, more than any other warning, made me want to stay as far away from sex as possible.

I value my relationship with Christ and my walk with Christ. Even as a teenager, I took it very seriously. While most of my friends were listening to secular music, I listened to gospel CDs. When I got my first car, I played Yolanda Adams's *Mountain High . . . Valley Low* album till I wore it out! I almost never turned on the radio. The thought of allowing myself to engage in simple, *normal* teenage activities (and when I say *simple,* I mean things like having a crush on a boy) was scary for me. I didn't understand that these were just part of adolescence. I viewed them as sinful, as attacks on my purity. It was my job to actively fight against my flesh to remain pure.

While a biblical sexual ethic for Christians is a noble and necessary goal, the core message of the purity movement is steeped in fear and shame that are disproportionately directed toward women. That shame made me fall victim to what I call the good-girl mentality, which became a core part of my identity. I remember watching a movie as a child in which a young woman tells her mother that she wants the first person she kisses to be the man she eventually marries. In my preteen mind, I decided this was a good strategy, a sign of what my life was to become. I was dead set on following that good-girl plan. Little did I know that I was setting myself up for a rough road in undoing that identity.

Kevin:

Christian boys got different messages about sex. While there was still plenty of shame, we were made to feel less bad about being sexually active. Out loud, parents discouraged their sons from having sex, but there was still plenty of "atta boy" unspoken approval. I heard a lot of men talk about all the womanizing they did before God delivered them or before they found a wife and got married. The dialogue went something like this: "Before I met my first lady and God put me here, I used to be out there—you understand me? Your man was out there. I had the suit; I had the women; I was the man!" The vibe was like a club of good old boys, and even the preachers would join in. But you never heard women talking about their wild lives before they found God. The rules were just different. Men were meant to pursue, to win women over, even if it sometimes went too far. Those messages of masculinity sat on the same level as, or even a little bit above, Christianity.

That being said, I wish that someone—anyone—would have kept it real. We knew that sex was taboo and that even thinking about sex was a big no-no. But teenage boys could have used a little realistic guidance about what to do with all our sexual thoughts and feelings. Here are the only instructions I got about dealing with those thoughts:

1. Pray.
2. Take a cold shower.
3. Pray again.
4. Read the Bible.

Okay, so now I'd prayed, taken a cold shower, prayed again, and read the Bible. And what happened throughout that time? I was horny. I had a hard peen while taking a cold shower. Standing there, I realized, *Hey, this water kind of feels good. I'm already here; I might as well finish what I started. I got body wash right here. Let me just turn the water up a bit.* I may have even slowed down a little when I was washing them old balls.

No matter how many times I repeated the instructions, the horniness didn't go away. The idea behind those instructions was this: The more time you spend with God, the less you think about sex. But the promise didn't deliver as advertised. I wanted a refund.

We were also taught that masturbation was wrong. Wrong. Wrong. Wrong. If you jack off, you're going to hell. But on *The Love Hour,* we've spoken to countless therapists and experts who teach that not only is it *not* wrong; it's an important part of your sex life. Masturbation is a building block, especially for women.

The first time I heard anything about masturbation that was different from the message drilled into my head was when a pastor debunked, scripturally, the idea that masturbation is wrong. He said that for married people to have a good, healthy relationship, each person should be able to tell their partner what they like. It's like in a restaurant, when a server asks for your order. It's your responsibility to know what you truly want: steak, shrimp, spicy food. When you get married, you need to know your preferences so you can tell your partner how to please you. That's a very different message from the one we were taught for twenty-five years.

Still, the purity movement didn't make teen boys like me feel that bad. Boys and girls received the same information but didn't bear the same shame. When I look back at it now, the part that did the most damage was the notion of power. As a guy, my job was to be a player and take someone's virginity. It was something to be conquered. It's crazy to think about now, but somehow at that time, this idea was cool. It was done in movies, on TV, by the guys I knew. It was the thing to do. Men dominated women in countless stories of conquest: from King Solomon and his seven hundred wives and three hundred concubines[1] to Def Jam's *How to Be a Player.* It was all the same.

When Melissa and I were newly married, some church friends of ours conceived. They weren't married, but everyone kinda knew they was bumping uglies. When the woman started showing, she was "sat down" from her duties in the church. She couldn't volunteer for any organizations, sing in the choir, stuff like that. The guy was the church drummer and also sang, but he wasn't sat down. He faced no punishment or additional shame. In some ways, knowing that sort of shame wouldn't befall me, even if I did get caught, made me more likely to fool around. And fool around I did.

I was careful, though. And the reason I was careful was not because of any lessons I learned in church. When I was thirteen, my sixteen-year-old brother did not have the testicular fortitude to tell our parents that he had gotten a girl pregnant, so he had me deliver the news to my mom. I still remember the reaction on my mom's face. From that day on, I watched my brother's life get more difficult rather quickly. His opportunities became very limited. Watching his life change because of this baby was probably the thing that made me fully understand the seriousness of sex and the potential consequences of being sexually active.

Promise #2

You Are Guaranteed a Healthy Sex Life After You Say "I Do"

Melissa:

Even though the words were never explicitly delivered, the lessons were constant—a little here, a little there, from parents and in church—that if I withheld from having sex just a little longer, my first time with my new spouse would move heaven and earth, and subsequently, my sex life with my spouse would always be healthy and satisfying. It's similar to the messages of masculinity Kevin absorbed over the years. Even though no one spelled it out explicitly, these were the truths we just knew from growing up churchy. My world was framed by these truths.

The fallout of this promise piggybacks on the first one about desirability and shame. If purity equals salvation, then the opposite is also true: Nonpurity means damnation. And the shame switch doesn't just flip as soon as you get married. I carried that negativity with me. Here I was, married, in a situation where I should be free. But in all scenarios relating to sex— talking about it, getting ready for it, doing it—I felt shame. It felt wrong. I still suffered from the good-girl syndrome. By this point, it was no longer about the messaging. I suffered from all that I had internalized; purity had become my key character trait.

I remember sitting in church next to my first boyfriend, the one I dated right before Kevin. The teen Bible had pages with vibrant colors, specifically designed to grab your attention. There was a sex page, a porn page, a drug page—all the dangers they wanted us to understand. This boyfriend opened to the sex page and pointed to the graphic and then pointed to the two of us. It was his far-from-subtle way of telling me we should have sex. I thought, *You mean to tell me we are in church, a man is preaching in front of us about the dangers of heavy petting and how fiery hot the lake of fire is, and this boy grabs my Bible and tells me we should have sex? This ain't never gonna work. Never. Ever.* That was the end of that relationship. I didn't date again until Kevin. I could not be tempted!

We concentrated so much on abstinence and the wait, but we were never taught what to do after that. No one taught you how to have a beautiful sex life with your partner. As a newly-wed, I felt betrayed, bamboozled, tricked. I did everything right and still struggled to accept my sexuality. I had to come to my own process of educating myself about my body, about sex (the way God intended it), and the beauty of two lives coming together. I now see my upbringing as a kind of brainwashing: Even when you're confronted with the truth, you still feel compelled to hold on to the lie.

After eighteen-plus years as a married woman, my good-girl syndrome still sticks to me like glue. I still feel compelled to do everything right, to cross every *t* and dot every *i*. I fight actively to keep this kind of thinking from bleeding into my sex life. Shame is difficult to overcome. As Donna Coletrane Battle, now a spiritual practitioner and a Duke Divinity School professor, said at the 2018 Courage Conference in Raleigh, North Carolina, "We can overcome trauma. It is shame that is so incredibly difficult to overcome . . . Shame goes directly to the heart of where we feel worth and value and it tears it; it rips it apart."[2]

Kevin:

We all need to be freer to talk about sex, and these conversations about sex need to happen on a regular basis. The problem is, we have made sex just plain awkward to talk about. The only conversation I had with my parents about the birds and the bees happened when I was nineteen years old and returned home from college for the weekend. It went something like this:

Mom: "Boy, are you a virgin?"
Me: "No."
Mom: "You're nasty."
[End of conversation]

But it doesn't have to be that way. And it shouldn't be. Parents and other people in authority think that by avoiding the conversation, kids aren't going to do it. But avoiding the conversation just teaches us to be embarrassed and uncomfortable around the subject of sex.

The conversation about sex isn't awkward only with parents or teachers or pastors. It can even be uncomfortable and embarrassing with your own spouse, the person with whom you are having, or wanting to have, all the sex.

Confession: Early in our marriage, I used to think that every time the sun went down, it meant I'd be having sex. I'm not joking. Shortly after our honeymoon, I said to Melissa, "It's dark outside; let's get to it. We have four years of celibacy to catch up on." Kudos to her for not making me feel dumb or bad about it, but she did say, "Yes, it is dark. Are you expecting sex just because the sun has gone down?" I thought, *I guess I can't say yes when she puts it that way. Maybe it's ridiculous to expect sex because it's dark.* But I still wanted to shout, "Yes!" I didn't know what to say or not say. I felt awkward with my own wife.

Another thing I did was expect sex just because we hadn't had it in a while. If it had been three or four days, I knew my chances improved with each passing day. I now know that I increase my chances of sex by making sure my wife and I are closely connected. That doesn't mean cooking dinner for her on and only on the nights I want butt. It means doing the things that fill our love tanks. Spending time with each other. Not just burning some burgers and saying, "Are you ready now?"

The promise of purity culture—that just because you're married, your sex life is going to automatically work—is an empty one. You have to talk about it, even though talking about sex is hard. The good news is, the more you talk about sex, the easier it gets. Make it normal. Make it a regular part of the conversations you have with your spouse.

Side note: It's probably a good idea to have these conversations separate from the actual act. If you're in the process of foreplay and you bring up what ain't working, you're going to ruin the mood. That's why we suggest talking about it when you're fully clothed or not even in the bedroom. Maybe in the car on the way to the grocery store, when you know you have only ten minutes for a quick check-in: "So, the butt stuff—where you at?"

You better get used to talking about sex with your partner. When you're married or in a long-term relationship, you're going to have to have the conversation more than you might think, because sex has phases. The phases change with adjusting to new jobs, having children, dealing with health issues, or just growing older. And the longer you're married, the more phases you're going to have. Remember, you might have sexual chemistry now, but that doesn't mean you always will. Many of life's phases bring stressors that could result in a sex slump, and when you're in a sex slump, you need to know that you'll get out of it. Remember, though, it may take some time. Let the feelings that come with new life phases take time to settle in, and then make an effort to bring sexual intimacy back to your relationship. Slumps in the bedroom, like slumps on the baseball field, end. But sometimes you have to adjust your swing.

Melissa:

Just recently, Kevin posted a joke about sex, and someone commented, "I miss righteous Kev." While I agree that there is a time and place for everything, I don't agree that righteousness is mutually exclusive from sexuality. I have been on a mission to close the gap between the two.

The best sex comes from first knowing yourself and then

revealing yourself. Your sex life, your pleasure, and your or-gasm are *your responsibility, not your partner's!* Yes, your spouse can help, but the hard work of really getting to know yourself has to be done on your own. This is not going to hap-pen in the act of having sex.

When we got married, I was a virgin and Kev was not. The result was that we had very different starting points when it came time to do the do. We weren't comfortable doing the same things, and it made for a difficult transition into married life. I didn't even have the words to talk about what I liked, what I wanted, and what I didn't want. Kevin had more experience, but he didn't know what I wanted, he didn't know my body, and neither of us was comfortable having the conversation.

But, y'all, we got past it, and you can too! For a couple to grow into a healthy space, the person with more experience or a more adventurous nature has to make sure that there is open, honest dialogue around all aspects of the act. Talk about what you want from your partner in specific terms. Talk about what you'd like to do with them, and make sure the pathways you describe are free of barriers. If one of you wants to change the direction, that shift needs to be discussed.

Another thing we've found is that it's really important that the person whose comfort level is in question be the one who is in control of the sexual momentum. No one wants to be in a position where they are made to feel uncomfortable. If one per-son pushes too hard, particularly with something that the other has said they are not comfortable with, it's going to create a lack of trust.

This is a good place to tell you about our stoplight method. The stoplight method is essentially a way of owning and de-claring your agency over your sexual activity. For instance, if you label certain behaviors or positions as green, you're saying that you're comfortable with those. Under yellow, you'd list the sex stuff that you might be okay with at some point—maybe not right now, but you think you'll be open to it in the future. If something is yellow, your partner knows that it needs to be discussed and approved before anyone gives it a try. Your feelings about it are still being worked out. If you talk about it beforehand, it might go from yellow to green, but if you betray the trust, it will likely go from yellow to red. The red category includes any and all sexual activity that you know you're definitely not interested in.

Greens and reds are very clear. With the yellows, it's a good idea to come up with a plan for moving them to green—or even red. "We tried this, and no thank you; let's go ahead and move that to red," or "I am now more comfortable with it, and it is green." Without these conversations, yellows stay in a perpetual state of limbo.

The stoplight method should be discussed early—even before the first time you and your partner have sex. From there, it should be a regular conversation at intervals throughout your relationship. By using the stoplight method, you establish trust and boundaries, which are especially important if one person in the relationship is more experienced and/or experimental than the other. This way, you have a road map, and the person who might be a little more hesitant trusts that their partner is not going to go off-roading.

We learned about the stoplight method thirteen years into our marriage. We wanted to spice some things up while maintaining trust. We started by having Kevin (the more adventurous) list all the things that he wanted to try in the bedroom. Anything and everything. Then together we went over what was okay with me (green), what was a possibility with further conversation (yellow), and what was a hard no (red). When we had our new list in front of us, we went on a European vacation, because the things that were more risqué seemed like a better idea across the pond. Away from our kids.

Interestingly, a lot of things we didn't think we would be comfortable doing ended up in the green and yellow categories. And since that list is ever-changing, periodic check-ins are also a good idea. I can't emphasize it enough: The key is trust. The red stays red. Pushing is not allowed. I will not hear, "Hey, can it be yellow? Just one time?" That kind of talk pokes holes in the trust.

When we talk about trust here, we are not talking about fidelity. This isn't about a fear of being cheated on. This trust is about believing that the boundaries a person has established around sex and their body will be respected and honored. If one person tries to push those boundaries, it's going to feel like trespassing. But where there is trust, there is intimacy and sexual freedom. And that's the good stuff; that's where the fun is.

Remember, the experience is supposed to be about pleasure, and pleasure is experienced differently by different people. So the dialogue is about expressing to your partner what you want to give, what you want to receive, and what turns you on.

Kevin:

We firmly believe that God did not want sex to be boring. If he did, he would not have given us the ability to do all these different things in the bedroom. He created sex for marriage. He wants us to spice it up!

At the beginning of our marriage, Melissa's and my sex life could best be described as simple. We approached all aspects of sex in the most basic ways. And it was fine for a while. In fact, the sex was great. But over the course of our eighteen-year marriage, our sex life has evolved in a lot of healthy ways. That's normal! Your sex life will be one way when you're newly married and will change as you go through those phases we talked about. You might have less sex when you're sleep deprived with a new baby. There likely will be no daytime sex when kids are running around the house. On the other hand, the confidence that comes with a promotion or a raise could give your libido a lift. The phase of life you're in has a huge impact on your sex drive, your sex life—all of it.

Now, in most of these life phases, there's going to be a sex-drive disparity. Sex is not like cleaning the kitchen or cooking dinner, which you can still do well even with a stink attitude. You don't have to be in a good mood to sweep the floor, but if your heart's not in it when you're trying to make sweet love, it has the opposite effect of what sex is supposed to accomplish, which is to satisfy a need and bring a couple closer together. You might think that the person with the lower desire should sometimes accommodate the other's needs—just suck it up and do it anyway. But that does not work. It's unfair to both people, and the result is trash sex.

Here are the facts. You and your partner are not always going to want sex at the same time, and it's next to impossible to turn down sex without making your partner feel rejected. When Melissa is not in the mood for sex, I make the mistake of thinking that we're the only couple having that disconnect— that the man feels wanted and desired every time he walks through the door at the end of the day. Of course, deep down I know that's not true. But in moments where I feel rejected, I assume that I'm the only man in the world whose wife is turning him down.

It's crucial to remember that not wanting sex is not the same thing as not wanting your partner. And the flip side: If your partner turns down sex, it doesn't mean they don't want and adore you. You can love your spouse and be super attracted to them without wanting to get naked and crazy every time they rub on your booty.

I can't say I have the perfect solution for how to turn down sex in a way that saves your partner's feelings and ego. For your spouse's confidence, do your very best to make them feel wanted. Remind them that you think of them in a sexual way: Maybe you make sexy little comments or gestures at random times, when they least expect it. That will go a long way to ease the tension when sex is turned down.

Melissa:

Sometimes simple willingness has the capacity to bring about horniness (for lack of a better word). In other words, if you aren't necessarily feeling it but you're willing, the desire often will follow.

It's like going to the gym. If my alarm wakes me up to go work out and I'm comfy and warm and cozy under my blankets, I don't want to get out of bed. I don't want to get dressed and put my sneakers on. But if I am willing, if I push myself to take those steps, I know I won't regret it. I know it will feel good both during and after my barre class. With sex, I might be tired, I might be comfortable, I might not feel the desire quite yet, but if I am willing, it's crazy how the feelings will often follow. If I take the initial steps of willingness, I know it will get hot and heavy. It will feel good both during and after.

Some people don't have spontaneous sexual thoughts. If they let that control their sexual activity or lack thereof, they will never have sex. Spontaneity is overrated anyway. You can get brainwashed to think that something is wrong with you and your relationship if you don't spontaneously tear your spouse's clothes off and push them down on the kitchen counter to ravage their body. In fact, movies and media have romanticized spontaneity and done damage to real people's sex lives, because we think if our desire doesn't look like what we see onscreen, then it's not good enough. Life is far more scheduled and routine than it is spontaneous.

Women are often not socialized to desire sex. Instead, historically speaking, we are socialized to *be desired*. But I've come to realize that I am entitled, I have a birthright, to desire. I was designed to be sexual and to seek and enjoy pleasure. I used to think, *It's my husband's responsibility to know me and my body and to figure out my turn-ons and turnoffs.* But I didn't even know what turn-ons and turnoffs were! Before I could rely on him to make me feel good, I had to work to get to know myself. I had to understand my body and my needs. We must take control and ownership of our sexuality! You have to learn what turns you on and off—or, as author and sex researcher Emily Nagoski calls them, your accelerators and your brakes.[3]

When Kevin and I discussed our accelerators and brakes, we saw, not surprisingly, that our lists were vastly different. It's a wonder we ever get down to business! In your relationship, you'll find that some things—a scent, a dirty house, stress at work—turn you off from the idea of sex. It's hard to get in the mood when your brakes are being pressed. Then there are your accelerators, your turn-ons.

Melissa's Accelerators	Kevin's Accelerators
Closeness	Nakedness
My own self-confidence	Smelling good (perfume)
Erotic talk throughout the day	Lingerie
	Days of the week
	Empty house
	Full house
	It really can be anything
Melissa's Brakes	**Kevin's Brakes**
Body odor	Being musty myself
Lack of closeness outside the bedroom	Recent pooping
Stress	
Dirty house	

It's your responsibility to know what turns you on so you can articulate those things to your partner. List your own accelerators and brakes, share them with your partner, and keep them current. Revisit what works for you and what doesn't. Check in with your spouse about their lists—and more importantly, take your partner's lists to heart. Pay attention to those pedals!

Promise #3

You Will Have a Fairy-Tale Marriage Because You Didn't Ruin Yourself by Having Multiple Sexual Partners

Kevin:

You can't just think, *Since I'm married, everything is going to be smooth and easy, and I can rest on that without any real effort*. Nope. It's kind of like life. You can check the boxes—go to college, study hard, get a job—and still not live the fairy tale. In college, I was working at a daycare making minimum wage, and even though I followed all the rules, I ended up at the same job with a thirty-cent raise. In the same way, I later realized that plenty of people who had premarital sex still have healthy marriages. Because they put in the work.

Melissa:

When we were newly married, I spent a lot of time making sense of things: If God made me and he says that I am good and I am a work of art, then why am I walking around in shame? If God sees me as a masterpiece, then why do I feel bad about my body and my sexuality? I had to get comfortable with all of that. I had to accept that I was now a married woman. I needed to know and appreciate my own body so that I could get comfortable with sex.

In church, you might have heard the verse that says, "Let the marriage bed be undefiled."[4] *Undefiled* here means "uncontaminated" or "set apart." We take that to mean you shouldn't invite other people's ideas, opinions, and judgments into your marriage bed. Don't let other people dictate to you what your sex life should look like. As our good friend Goody Howard says, "Don't let them yuck your yum." A lot of people will tell you what's right or wrong in terms of sex, but no one else knows what's right or wrong for your bedroom. Other people's opinions should not keep you from doing what feels right to you. So embrace your body. I suggest getting comfortable with your body by walking around the house naked. Go to bed naked. Get over the shame of nakedness.

Sex is for pleasure, and we all feel pleasure differently. No one wants to be unfulfilled, and no one wants their spouse to feel unfulfilled. Don't create rules for yourself and your marriage to the detriment of your relationship. Don't keep yourself from exploring due to some assumed religious obligation.

Kevin:

When things aren't great in your current sexual relationship and you get into a slump or get insecure about your desirability, you might be tempted to remember a previous partner, where that specific thing you're currently struggling with wasn't a problem. But remember, that's no longer an option. You have to do the work with the person you're with now! You should always be working toward happiness in your sexual relationship—happiness for you *and* your partner. Through communication, you can move forward and out of scenarios that provide discomfort in the bedroom.

In every marriage, one person is going to have the higher sex drive. Sometimes it's a woman, sometimes a man, but either way, the disparity can create distance between you if you're not careful. No matter who it is, it's important to acknowledge that you are just wired differently.

The incredible Dr. Laurie Watson uses the terms *pursuer* and *distancer*.[5] In our relationship, I am the pursuer. The honest truth is that I am thinking about sex constantly. I think about how likely I am to have sex in the near future. I think about when, where, and how. I plot out my week. If Liss starts her period on a Monday, I do some calculations and think maybe I can have sex by Friday.

As we sit and write this book, it's a nice, sunny Monday afternoon. I am thinking, *We didn't have sex last night because we were both exhausted. I've got to watch a documentary for a podcast tomorrow, and Melissa and I need to watch a movie that we're reviewing on another podcast later this week. We are getting haircuts tonight, and Jojo has soccer. Not to mention, our friend usually comes over to watch* The Bachelor, *which ends at ten P.M. Sometimes she and Melissa talk until one A.M., so my chances for butt butt tonight are very low. However, the next day's forecast looks good, since we are doing a little staycation without the kids this weekend.*

I can be completely asleep, dead to the world, yet the slightest suggestion of sex can get me awake, alert, and ready. If Liss gets up to go to the bathroom in the middle of the night, I'm ready to go. Or maybe I'm in the kitchen and it happens to be one of the few moments when I'm not thinking about sex. If Liss brushes past me, all of a sudden, I'm thinking about sex. She probably doesn't even mean anything by it, but it's instant caveman mode. Sex comes first. Then food. Then sleeping.

In year seventeen of our marriage, we both had moments when we learned about each other and our levels of desire. For Melissa, after many years of being lower desire and even some instances where she acted emotionally superior for not needing sex, something changed. We had been going through a rough patch, and I was traveling a crazy amount. After a couple weeks of little to no sex, Melissa realized she needed the physical connection and began initiating it. For me, the learning curve was realizing that the most effective foreplay for Melissa was actually emotional connection: long talks, vulnerability, check-ins after we'd been separated for extended periods of time. All of that led to a desire to be physically intimate, and oh, what a realization it was.

When it comes to any and all sex, I have an attitude of gratitude. God has given us the gift of sex, which I think means we have license to be freaky.

Speaking of freaky, we cannot have a chapter about sex without covering a few other items. Let's start with oral sex. I have encountered lots of churchy folks who ask me if I think oral sex is a sin. The answer is no. A sin is a transgression that separates you from God. Oral sex does not separate us from God. In fact, sometimes it makes you thank him in the moment! The parameters for your sex life are set by asking yourself two questions:

1. Are you both comfortable?
2. Do you both agree?

If the answer to both questions is yes, go get after it. Same with videoing your sex. As far as I'm concerned, that's game film. You want to be the best player you can be. Enjoy the freedom to love your spouse and find the things you guys are open to. Go nuts. It's more dangerous to be on different planes in terms of what you're willing to try. Don't leave stuff unexplored. Lewis and Clark it. Give yourself a chance to see what you like. Otherwise you're just pumping and licking in the dark.

Melissa:

Let me go back to what Kevin was saying about the fact that in most marriages one person is higher and the other is lower desire. To the lower-desire people, I get you! It is so difficult to understand how important sex is to someone when it simply isn't that important to you. Okay, I got that off my chest. Thank you.

I have a piece of advice—two simple words, in fact—that will help solve a variety of issues in the bedroom: vacation sex. There's just something about getting away from your house, where the laundry basket is full and the dishwasher needs to be unloaded and the kids are right in the next room, that frees your mind for healthier, more relaxing, more fun sex. It doesn't have to be Hawaii or the Bahamas; it can be a little hotel the next town over. For me, it's all about detaching from the stressors in your everyday life. It's truly amazing what a change of scenery can do for your libido. Being on vacation is one of my most dependable accelerators.

You Should Know

You'd think, given all our research and conversations, that nothing would be left unsaid between us, that we are totally open to each other and understand each other's every sexual need. That just isn't the case. We're still human and we're still married, which means we do not get everything right. Even with all the work we do, things are still left unsaid.

And here's the thing: Sometimes we don't want to *have* to say those things. There are ideas and feelings that we want our spouses to know instinctively, particularly in the bedroom.

That's marriage, though. So much of it is spent figuring out what your spouse likes and wants. What your spouse knows about you one day might be a little different the next. And if you assume they have direct access into your brain, you're going to be disappointed. You remember the old adage about what happens when you assume, right? You make an "ass" out of "u" and "me." Yep. Those are the facts. Assuming your partner knows what you're thinking puts you both in a bad spot.

The "you should know" pitfall is a danger to any sexual relationship. Kev might assume that Melissa knows he wants to have sex every time he enters the bedroom (or any room for that matter). Melissa thinks Kev should know that she needs a longer runway to get there, especially when she's stressed or had a long day. If we're both operating on the principle that our partner should just know, we're going to stall out and create resentment.

You might think your spouse should know that when your in-laws are in town, sex is off the table. We caution you to make sure you're communicating what you want your spouse to know. Even if you've said it before. A hundred times. You should know that your spouse probably doesn't know what you're thinking or how things make you feel. And it costs you nothing to tell them.

Melissa:

The thing that falls under the "you should know" category for me is that I think Kev should know what is necessary for me to be in the mood. I need to feel intimacy, and I often think he should know what that requires. For me, intimacy is spelled t-i-m-e and t-a-l-k. I require quality time and conversation in order to be intimate. Sex, for me, is more emotional than physical. Sexual desire is a direct reflection of my emotional connection. If I'm not feeling emotionally close to Kevin, my sexual desire will be limited. I want Kevin to make an effort to connect with me on an emotional level, through conversation and non-sexual touch. If I don't feel emotionally connected, I might commit my body to meet Kev's sexual needs, but if I'm being 100, that makes me feel used. He might recognize that I'm not feeling connected and merely along for the ride, which has the potential to make him feel rejected. So, what I wish he knew is that his emotional connection to me not only helps me enjoy sex; it makes sex better for him too.

Sometimes Kev's touch serves only to foreshadow what he's expecting to happen in the bedroom. Don't touch me only when you want sex. If Kev touches me during the day simply because he's thinking of what he wants that night, I learn to take his touch as less about affection and more about foreplay. And I appreciate nonsexual affection. I want Kev to know that sometimes I resent his touch because I know it's only about wanting something from me later.

Kevin:

I spell intimacy as s-e-x. For me, once my body is ready for sex, my mind follows, no matter what was on my mind before we got going. I know when Melissa isn't into it. She might mean well and give it up. I appreciate that, and I will take it, but I know when she's not into it. In some ways, it's worse than saying no to sex.

When she rejects sex, I feel like she's rejecting me personally. I'm fragile. I was not taught how to express my feelings to a woman. To this day, I don't know how to express myself when I'm feeling that rejection. Even writing those words right now makes me feel weak.

I want to feel wanted. I don't always want to be the initiator of sex. I don't want to always be the one, even though 99.9 percent of the time, it's me who goes after it. It makes me feel like a little dog whining for a treat. I mean, you might give it to him, but you're a little annoyed when you do. I don't always want to ask for the draws; I want the draws to be offered up. I need to feel wanted. My sexual connection with Melissa is tied to my feeling worthwhile as a man. If I have sex seven days in a week, nothing will bother me that week: traffic jams, pay cuts, weight gain. I could catch on fire and it wouldn't bother me because Melissa wanting me gives me all the confidence I need.

Surprise me. Rub my leg while I'm sleeping. Melissa loves when I surprise her with flowers or edible arrangements; it makes her feel like I'm thinking of her in a romantic way. I want to be surprised and reminded that she thinks of me in a sexual way. If Melissa walks into the room wearing lingerie and she is not wearing a bonnet on her head, I'm gonna be like, "No bonnet? Is it my birthday? Is she wanting sex from me? Does she desire me?" That will do wonders for me. I will wake up the next morning ready to attack the world.

Relationship Check-In

We suggest that you and your partner have regular sex check-ins. After you've read and taken in all the information in the previous pages, it may be a good idea to have a conversation together.

Ask yourself and each other these questions:

- What are your stoplights?
- What are your boundaries?

- What are your accelerators and brakes?
- How are you feeling about your agency?
- How are you feeling in your body?
- What emotions are all these questions eliciting for you?

Chapter Four

Jealousy Be Hard

Before we launch into a whole chapter about jealousy, we are going to do that thing we love to do: provide a definition. For the purposes of this conversation, we are going to classify *jealousy* as "thoughts and feelings of insecurity, fear, and anxiety of an anticipated loss of something of great personal value."

No one likes that jealous feeling. It can make you queasy. But it isn't always a bad thing. In fact, we think there are two types of jealousy, differentiated by the emotions that bring it on. The first is jealousy born of love. This is the jealousy that God feels over us, the kind that comes from seeing an actual threat to your relationship. The second form is jealousy born from insecurity. This type of jealousy arises out of suspicion, even though there might be no real threat or even evidence of a threat.

Melissa:

In the last chapter, we discussed how your sex life changes as you and your marriage go through changes. Same goes for your jealous responses. Depending on where you are emotionally, physically, and mentally, you will react to situations with more or less jealousy.

In the third year of our marriage, we were going through some major transitions. Kevin was launching his comedy career at a time when I was reeling from my parents' divorce. (More on that in chapter 10, "Divorce Be Hard.") I was questioning everything in my life, and my reactions to Kev in that season were definitely informed by my new sense of insecurity. I was an exposed nerve, and his new life was hitting that nerve at every turn.

Kevin was developing his talent, so every Thursday, he would go out to a nightclub and work on new jokes and material. While he spent his nights out at these clubs, I was stuck at home with two small boys. And remember, we grew up churchy (as if you could ever forget), so this whole club thing was foreign to us.

Well, it turns out Kevin was getting himself quite a fan base, a group of women who were a little clique of friends. Facebook's tagging feature was new at the time, and all of a sudden, while Kevin was out and I was home, I started to see photos of Kevin with women I didn't know. And the clothes these women were wearing to the club were unlike anything I had in my closet. I was seeing them in sexy tops and short skirts, all up close and personal with my husband. They coined the hashtag #KevsNumberOneFan and #KevsGroupieNotGroupie. On the heels of my parents' divorce, these posts were making me feel a certain kind of way. But I did not have as honest a conversation with Kevin as I should have because I feared coming off as a jealous wife.

I was upset, but instead of confronting Kevin when he got home, I just went to bed. And I went to bed mad. It's not that I didn't want to deal with Kevin; the truth is, I didn't want to deal with my own emotions. Another factor at play was that I knew all too well that Kevin, my husband, has a philosophy he holds dear: *You're either with me or against me.* (More on that in chapter 5.) Even the slightest inclination of a doubt or a problem would be interpreted as me taking a stance against his dream. So I slept it off. In the morning, I told myself, *I trust Kevin. It's not that big of a deal, and it will be okay. It's a new morning and all that stuff was yesterday.*

I wish I could go back in time and make sure we had a productive discussion about it, because by the time we did talk about it, I had been holding too much in for too long. The reckoning happened in two stages. The first was a blowup after I had been holding my jealousy in for six months. Six months of pictures, posts, tags, and mounting anger. Also, Kevin was doing a "look good, feel good" thing, and he would take his shirt off onstage every chance he got. But I didn't say a word about any of it until I lost it over a game of Twitter Taboo.

Here's how it went down. Every Thursday night, Kevin went to a show that started at ten p.m. On this particular Thursday evening, he ate before the rest of the family so he could make it to the club early. All afternoon, we didn't really connect on any level, deep or shallow, not because we were beefing but because we were busy and that's how it often went. I came home after a long day at work, I cooked and cleaned up a bit, I bathed the boys and got them ready for bed, and before I had a chance to catch my breath, Kevin was out the door to the comedy club. Kevin gave me a kiss goodbye (which was a kiss good night since I went to sleep while he was out) and then rushed out to the club.

Thirty minutes later, I saw this tweet from him: "Who wants to play a game of Twitter Taboo?" He then set up a virtual game of Taboo on Twitter and played for an hour or so before his set, and he kept it going after he got offstage. Here's what I was thinking: *My husband misses the opportunity to connect with me over dinner and rushes out to a club while I stay home with our kids so he can achieve his dreams. And he's using that time to connect with thousands of strangers?* It was infuriating. That game of Taboo was the catalyst for a long-overdue discussion about all of it.

The truth is, I didn't even really understand what was bothering me. All I knew at the time was that I felt Twitter was getting more from Kevin than I was. I cried, and we talked, and Kevin agreed not to play Taboo on Twitter. But that didn't resolve the real issue, which was that we were not connecting. In conflicts, we tend to address the wound but not its cause. It's like putting a Band-Aid on your knee when you have internal bleeding. We made that mistake: fixing big problems with the scaffolding of our relationship. And the deal with scaffolding is, it's temporary, designed to keep things in place while the real structural work is done. But we were relying on the scaffolding to hold our marriage together.

The more productive conversation came in year seventeen of our marriage, when we were more educated about communication and open to being vulnerable. That's when we had a real talk about the feelings that created jealousy and insecurity all those years ago. By the time we had that conversation, the Twitter Taboo issue was not an isolated incident. It was fourteen years of those types of scenarios—times when I felt hurt and wronged, times when resentment built up. It was also fourteen years of personal growth and development that allowed for that productive conversation about jealousy.

Kevin:

Boundaries were being crossed for sure, but I was oblivious. People would come to the comedy show dressed for the club, and when the comedy show wrapped up, the twerking would commence. You know how people dress when they're going to a club—them thangs be thanging, booty and hips and thighs and titties were bouncing. And my ego was being served up for real. I mean, it seemed that just minutes before, I was a nobody, and then all of a sudden, people were recognizing me on the street. "Hey, man, you're that dude from the comedy show!" People came up to me in Safeway. I had fans for the first time in my life. It fed my ego.

In high school, I played one year of varsity basketball and had only one game where I scored more than twenty points. Let me explain something about our high school: We had guys on our teams who went pro, so those of us who weren't of that caliber were essentially nobodies. When I started in stand-up and was doing well, I had a great set and was the belle of the ball. People showed up just for me the way people in high school showed up to watch the stars on our team. In my mind, these were signs that my career was headed in the right direction. It hit particularly hard given that I was coming off a time when my income had dropped to nothing. Not making money killed my ego and my sense of what it meant to be a man. Being recognized and having fans fed that part of me.

All these factors informed how I handled the fan-club scenario. For me, it wasn't about the women. I didn't think about them in the sexual sense; they were signs that I was building my fan base. The idea was, the more pictures I got tagged in, the more people would follow me on social media or show up to see me perform. I was not thinking of Melissa's feelings. I was focused on whether I had a good show. I was blinded by the work of building up my social media following. I wasn't paying attention to how that affected my marriage or my wife.

Melissa:

We sometimes make the mistake of associating jealousy only with insecurity. We think that being jealous is a reflection of a low sense of self, not a valid awareness that our boundaries are being invaded. If we don't want to be labeled as a jealous person, we force ourselves to get over it. Or maybe we just pretend we're okay with a behavior that is not okay. There's a thin line between insecurity and justified jealousy, and that line often gets blurred.

For me, at the time this all went down, I was feeling slightly resentful. I was working in a bank all day and staying home with our kids at night. Kev wasn't working a day job, and he spent his nights out in a scene I didn't know or understand. Not only that, but he was also buying new clothes and new shoes for his fun nights out at the club. Meanwhile, I'm feeling like a frumpy new mom in my bank outfits. That was not what I signed up for.

Again, your marriage goes through phases, and whether or not you respond to behavior with jealousy is a product of the phase you're in. I was in an insecure place, so my jealousy was at an all-time high.

Kevin:

Let's go back a little further in time. Early in our marriage, I was working at the bank during the day and doing plays at night. Melissa had been our stage manager, but she retired from that role when the boys were born. She was no longer intricately connected to that part of my life, and, as she admits above, it fed her insecurities, which made us see things differently. All of this led to an incident that taught us both about healthy jealousy.

On BlackBerry Messenger (that shows you how long ago this was), I would chat with everybody that worked together on the plays. One woman I worked with happened to be someone I knew from high school and, truth be told, had had a little crush on. Okay, fine, a *big* crush. Okay, fine—back then, I was too unsure of my game to properly holla at her, and because Melissa and I were friends and not dating yet, I would talk about this girl to Liss, which probably ended up being a factor in the story I'm about to tell. The plays we performed were in Seattle, forty-five minutes from where we lived in Tacoma, and a bunch of us, including this woman, carpooled. To make matters worse, we had a new baby, and Liss stayed home with him most evenings.

The first incident happened at my birthday party. It was a potluck at our house, so everyone was bringing food: chips, salad—you get the idea. This woman, the one from the plays and the high school crush, brought a cake. And not just any cake but a homemade, not-from-a-box birthday cake. It was one of those individual-sized layer cakes with vanilla frosting and "Happy Birthday" spelled across the top in fancy icing. As soon as she arrived at the party, she told everyone how she had ruined the cake on her first attempt, went back to the grocery store, got all new ingredients, and made a second one. She was also showing people at the party that she had a burn on her arm from baking the cake.

My friends saw the problem right away. My brother and my friend pulled me outside to my car and were like, "Are you crazy? A girl bringing a cake that she baked? Not that she bought from Safeway for nine dollars? You're in big trouble. Melissa is going to take your life away."

And I was like, "What, what?" Totally oblivious. I didn't really think about the difference between one of my homegirls bringing spaghetti and this girl (the one that Melissa knew I used to have a crush on) bringing a birthday cake.

My brother had to hit me over the head: "Birthday cake is your wife! She does the cake. Not another woman."

Liss was livid, but to her credit, she kept it cool throughout the party. We actually have a picture of me and Melissa doing karaoke that night, and you'd never know from looking at the photo that she had fire inside. When the last person left, she closed the door, turned the lock, and put the chain on. And before that chain settled, she turned to me and said, "How could you? Why does she think it's okay to bring a just-for-you birthday cake? What have you been saying and doing to make her think this is okay?"

Once again, I was oblivious: "What, me? Done? I didn't do nothin'. I don't know what this girl was thinking. This is beyond me." The funny thing was, I didn't even like birthday cake, especially icing.

Even after the cake incident, this woman was still in my carpool to the theater for the plays we performed. We would text about what time we were leaving, who was driving, and what the plans were for the day or the week. But as Liss pointed out later, the communication between me and this woman went above and beyond the necessary logistics.

A few weeks after my birthday party, Melissa checked my phone. There was a message chain with this woman that had started when she thought she left her wallet in my car and wanted me to see if I could find it. However, the most recent message, the one Melissa saw, just said, "Black, Kenneth Cole. Thanks." Liss thought that I had complimented the woman's perfume and that she was responding, saying the perfume was called Black by Kenneth Cole.

Liss finally spoke up. "This contact is feeling very inappropriate," she said. "I don't like what's going on here. I'm uncomfortable."

Luckily, I cared far more about my wife and my marriage than I did about this woman. When Melissa voiced her feelings, I realized how far this situation had gone and I knew that it had to end. Quickly. I realized how badly the whole thing had hurt Melissa, and I knew it couldn't continue. Not for one minute.

I said, "I don't care about this girl. I care about you and this marriage. If you're this uncomfortable, I will end it. And that will be it."

The problem is that I didn't say anything to this other woman about cutting it off. I just went quiet, figuring she'd get the picture. A few days later, I got a message from her that said, "What, no 'good morning'?" Melissa saw it and told me I had to be clear to her about cutting it off. I then told this woman straight up that I couldn't talk to her anymore. She got so mad. She went off, saying that it sucks that single women can't have friends because married women always take it wrong. Liss was enraged and threw the phone at me. I had never seen her so upset.

In that moment, I was reminded that Melissa comes from a hot-blooded family. I had heard stories of her relatives fighting at funerals and baby showers, pregnant women punching and kicking each other. I had never seen that side of Melissa, but when she threw that BlackBerry, I saw that she was indeed from Toledo and had her mama's blood. In the years since, I have never seen her get that mad again. That's how I knew I had really messed up. For her to lose her cool like that made it simple: I had to cut things off with the girl.

Melissa:

The funny thing was, after the Kenneth Cole message, when I told Kevin I was uncomfortable with the whole thing, I still worried that I had acted like a jealous wife. I couldn't even bring myself to tell Kevin that I wanted him to cut off communication with the woman. I tempered it by asking that he scale it back . . . a lot. The come-to-Jesus moment for me was the day she commented that Kev had yet to wish her a good morning. That was a definite sign that he'd been talking to her too much. This was not jealousy born of insecurity. This was jealousy born out of love. This woman was an actual threat to my relationship. (On the other hand, more recently, when some porn star started following Kev on Twitter and making comments, I didn't care at all. Not one bit. I knew she was not an actual threat to this marriage.)

Kevin didn't give me any pushback about ending his friendship with the woman who baked him a cake. I'm glad I didn't have to work to convince him that severing ties was the right thing to do. Real problems arise when someone won't end a friendship outside their marriage when that friendship makes their partner uncomfortable. No relationship should be more important than your marriage. That's the kind of thing that will ignite suspicion.

Personal history and baggage from previous relationships often creep up in situations like these. Maybe your ex cheated on you and you brought that pain to your current relationship. Or maybe you had a friend make a move on your man and it left you more sensitive to and jealous of any behavior that verges on similar territory. It's important to know your partner and their history and work hard to validate their feelings. Even if nothing is going on and the friendship in question is completely innocent, if you're asked to cut it off, you do it to show your spouse that your marriage means more to you than a friendship. You never know: There might be an occasion where the tables turn and you'll want your spouse to do the same for you.

Marriage is like anything else you have that's valuable—you protect it. If you have jewelry or a cherished collectible, you do everything you can to keep it safe. Maybe you hide it or wrap it in bubble wrap. You do what you can so that thing of value isn't broken or tampered with. You make sure no outside force can penetrate it and decrease its value. It's the same with your relationship. Wrap your marriage in bubble wrap. Twice.

For Kevin and me, these steps we take to protect our marriage not only help us feel more secure in our relationship, but they also remind us that our spouse feels protective over us. We all want to be valued and adored, and that's why there is such a thing as healthy jealousy. When you speak up and let your partner know that you're feeling jealous, that your sensors are alerted and you want to keep the relationship safeguarded from a potential threat, it just might make your partner feel treasured. By the same token, your spouse could get a little perturbed if you're not jealous enough—and I speak from experience on that one.

A few years into our marriage, Kevin and I worked at Boeing, and a guy in the office was blatantly hitting on me. At first, it didn't bother me. I pretty much ignored him and his comments. That is, until the day I was wearing a sundress and this guy came up to me and said, "I should do an FOD check on you in that dress." For clarification, FOD stands for foreign object debris. An FOD check is a thorough scan of a plane for anything—a pen cap, an earring—that can compromise the integrity of the plane. Essentially, this co-worker was saying that he wanted to feel me up. I was ashamed and angry.

I came home that night and told Kev about it, expecting him to match my level of fury—or, even better, take it to the next level. After all, this co-worker was talking about doing a meticulous search in and around my dress. But Kev showed practically no emotion. He was in complete control, doing his best to validate my feelings instead of getting angry. It made me think he didn't care. I thought he should scream for this guy to be fired immediately or at least show a little healthy jealousy.

Let's go back to our definition. In this scenario, something Kevin considered to be of great personal value—his marriage—was being threatened. A boundary was being crossed. But no, he barely reacted.

Kevin:

Let me start by saying that God is jealous, and I want to be like God. But that's beside the point. There are two reasons that explain why I underreacted there.

The first is embarrassing, but I have to cop to it: I didn't know what an FOD check was. Yes, I worked at Boeing, but my job did not require me to get anywhere near airplanes. I typed into Excel spreadsheets for a living. The only reason I ever did see planes is because the café with the best snacks was located where the planes were made. Also, Boeing has a stupid number of acronyms. If I had known what an FOD check meant, I would have gone ballistic on that guy.

The other reason I underreacted relates to a story that serves as an important building block in the jealousy department of our marriage. A few years earlier, when Melissa was working at the bank, she had a co-worker who was talking to her crazy.

Melissa called and told me about a ridiculously inappropriate email from this guy, and I took that to mean I should do something about it. I told Melissa that my brother and I were clocking out of our jobs early to head over to the bank to beat that guy to the ground. I thought she was going to love it. I felt like a strapping, muscular prince, shirtless on a white horse, swooping in to save my damsel in distress. I would defend her honor and beat up this dude so that everyone at that branch would know: Don't nobody ever talk to my wife like this!

Melissa did not react with the gratitude I expected. She reminded me that I would go to jail, she would get fired, and the plan was dumb from start to finish. Turns out she had called me just to vent about this guy, not for me to come save her. So, later, when the FOD-check thing went down, I remembered how the last time something like this happened with a guy at Melissa's work, she made it very clear that she had it under control. Instead of freaking out, I downplayed it. My brain went through the process of telling me, *Last time you were jealous, she did not like your response, so you'd better not get as upset this time. If you flip out again, it will look like you didn't pay attention to her feelings.* What looked to Melissa like me not caring was really me trying too hard to learn from my mistakes. (And it didn't help that I had no idea what an FOD check was!)

At the end of the day, I had the right response to the wrong situation and the wrong response to the right situation. I even got jealous when Carlos, a seventy-five-year-old colleague of Melissa's, brought her homemade tacos and enchiladas that his wife had made. Melissa thought I was crazy. She said, "He's old enough to be my grandfather. Seriously, cut it out." A word to you men out there: You're usually going to be wrong whether you overreact or underreact. Therefore, my advice is to always overreact—then you'll be right at least 50 percent of the time.

Keep the energy up, but be careful to make sure your actions are warranted.

Over the course of a twenty-plus-year relationship, people are going to change, and your reactions to events and behavior are going to shift. It's important to love the current version of your spouse and pay attention to what they're going through. I always want my wife to be happy and feel safe. When Melissa asked me to ease up on the photos with groupies, we could have had an argument where I reminded her that I was working to do what was best for my brand. But my wife's feelings were more important. Even if I had no interest in the women she worried about, at the end of the day my goal is to have a safe, happy, comfortable relationship with my wife, which means I'm going to do what's good for her and for our marriage.

In a healthy marriage, you stay mindful of your behavior—not because it's right or wrong but because you're so tapped into where your spouse is emotionally and psychologically that you know how they're going to feel about your behavior. I see a lot of people who play stuff down and make their spouse's jealousy seem ridiculous with comments like "You're trippin'; you're trippin'." And my feeling is, even if they are trippin', you're setting the stage for jealousy and feeding that awful feeling when you should be building trust. It's a matter of priorities.

In both situations where my behavior or cluelessness contributed to Melissa's jealousy, I made adjustments to accommodate Melissa's feelings. If my career had to grow more slowly to keep my marriage intact, that was going to have to be okay. I didn't quit my comedy career to accommodate her feelings, because then I would have resented her for making me give up on my dream. But I changed my behavior because it was better for my marriage. And it wasn't that hard. In the end, things seem to be working out, both at home and onstage.

Melissa:

My friend Danni uses a phrase that perfectly suits this conversation: "Choose us." Kevin's shift in his routine was an example of his choosing us. When you are choosing us, the result might not be the exact thing that either of you wants, but it's what is best for the partnership, for the current situation that exists between the two of you. The key is to match your partner's reaction and to recognize where the jealousy is born: Out of love? Out of insecurity? Out of fear of losing something of great personal value? Identify what is at stake, where the feelings are coming from, and act accordingly.

Relationship Check-In

We've all had moments of jealousy, whether born out of love or insecurity. Both are valid feelings. Here are some questions to ask yourself and your partner as you work through this dynamic in your relationship:

- Do you feel your relationship is protected from being penetrated by outside forces? If not, why not?
- Is there a person who makes you feel jealous? Have you told your spouse? Are boundaries being crossed, or are you insecure? Should your spouse cut that person out?
- Is there something you can ask your partner to do to prevent you from feeling jealous in the future?

Chapter Five

Marital Roles Be Hard

There are countless surprises in any relationship, and writing this chapter took the two of us by surprise. The intention was to examine how having kids changed our marriage, but that's not what this chapter ended up being about. Not at all. It ended up exploring the different roles each of us has taken at different points of our marriage. Those roles have shifted, and sometimes—certainly in our case—they weren't the ones we originally signed on for.

After the birth of a child, most couples experience changes in their sex lives, their work-life balance, and the dividing and conquering of parenting tasks. And these changes can cause a lot of conflict. But when our first son, Isaiah, was born two years into our marriage, that was not where the struggle lay. Oh, we had a struggle all right, but it had nothing to do with the baby. We both changed diapers, we were both madly in love with our newborn son, and we respected how the other took on the job of parenting. The big challenge had nothing to do with sleep deprivation or diapers or burping. The struggle was about the roles we played, both at home and in the world.

As psychotherapist Esther Perel says, "When you pick a partner, you pick a story, and then you find yourself in a play you never auditioned for."[1] We know a couple who had to make adjustments when the wife's career skyrocketed. Her husband put his job lower on the priority list to support her and their kids. When they got married, they couldn't have foreseen that future, so they never thought to discuss those what-ifs. And even though they're in great shape financially because she just keeps getting raises, he goes back and forth between being proud of her and feeling inadequate as a man. He had to figure out how to take on a different role, and sometimes it's been a bumpy ride.

You know what they say: Life is what happens when you're making other plans. You're in it for the long haul, so you have to learn to pivot and adjust to the circumstances that unfold. Who knows? The role you end up playing might make you happier than the one you had in mind.

Melissa:

We had been married for only two years when I got pregnant unexpectedly. I was on the pill, but I really should have used a different form of birth control. I have an aversion to popping pills, maybe because addiction runs in my family. In fact, after my C-section, I wouldn't even take the painkillers my doctors prescribed. With my birth control pills, I often skipped a day or two or five—and then took a whole bunch and hoped it would do the trick. It did not.

Kevin and I had gone to Jamaica on our first cruise, and I expected my period while we were on the ship. I was as regular as clockwork, so when I missed my period, my first thought was that I must have miscounted or had the date wrong. As soon as I checked the calendar and determined that I did not get it wrong, I got nervous and scared. When we got home, I bought about five pregnancy tests—the thirty-dollar ones from CVS and the cheap ones from the dollar store. A blue line would show up, indicating a positive test, and I would try another one to see if the result might be different.

The night we found out about the pregnancy, I cried my eyes out. Kev was on the phone calling his family and friends while I sobbed. Those tears were about the fact that I was a checkbox person and the boxes were not checked, not even close. I was not, in any way, ready to start a family. In my mind, we needed more financial security, a real house, and money in the bank. I didn't feel we were in a position to provide. I kept repeating, "This isn't my plan."

I wish I could go back in time and not cry when I found out about the pregnancy. It hurt Kevin, and it is easily one of my biggest regrets. It's not that I didn't want my son—it's just that I wanted this baby to have the best possible life, and I didn't feel I could offer it at the time.

Kevin:

Melissa's crying broke my heart. I was excited to spread the good news, to tell the world that we were having a baby. I had dreamed of that moment, and I was excited to share it with her. It crushed me that our emotional responses were so opposite. I thought starting a family would be a dream come true, but it landed on us like a nightmare.

I knew Melissa's tears were not tears of joy, because she went into the bedroom and closed the door. I took her tears personally, even though none of the things she said were directed at me. Her tears, in my mind, revealed the fact that she had no faith in me, in my career, in my future. I thought it meant that she didn't want to have kids with *me*.

Despite that initial reaction, the nine months of pregnancy were smooth as silk. Melissa loved being pregnant. She got thick in all the right places, and she even loved that. The two of us were in lockstep, except for the time she was craving rib tips. We were in bed watching TV, and a commercial came on for Famous Dave's. Melissa said she wanted ribs, but I didn't move a muscle. It was 9:39 p.m. Famous Dave's closed at 10:00, and it was pouring rain. She turned to me and said, "You mean you won't go out and get me ribs? Look what I'm doing for you. Carrying your child. All I ask is for some rib tips." I drove through that rain and got her those ribs, and you know what? I was glad. I ate mine in the car and acted like I hadn't gotten any for myself. They were delicious.

Then the baby was born, and it was like going from traveling in the same car to being in separate lanes on the highway. For the first time, Melissa and I went from doing everything together to going our separate ways. Before we had the boys, we worked on plays together. And keep in mind, those plays were the most important thing in my life. They were the train tracks to my future. We were going to follow in Tyler Perry's footsteps, starting with plays in Seattle, then touring those plays, then making big successful movies, and Melissa was involved in it all. As stage manager, she made the whole operation work—more than the director, more than the actors, more than me. It's a tough job, and she was so good at it, and we all respected her. Even after she was no longer our stage manager, she would come and watch rehearsals, just to be where I was.

That's how our relationship had always worked. In high school, Melissa came to all my basketball games, and I went to all her track meets. In fact, I became the manager of her track team just so I could ride the bus with her to the meets. All through high school and college, we took classes together even though we had different interests and different majors. We always found a way to be in each other's space.

When Isaiah was born, something changed. Melissa immediately turned into the world's greatest mother, to the point where I would get a little jealous. When Isaiah was just a few months old, he was getting chronic ear infections, and Melissa did a bunch of research even before we took him to a specialist. She pre-diagnosed him, recognizing that he probably needed ear tubes. As usual, she did all the heavy lifting, and all I had to do was drive him to the doctor. If five things needed to be done to make sure the parenting stuff was handled perfectly, Melissa did four and a half, and I got to swoop in at the end and put a cherry on top.

One day when Isaiah was an infant, Melissa came to watch rehearsal, and she brought the baby in his car seat. It was pouring rain, she had worked a full shift at the bank that day, and she was there for no reason other than to show up for me. After that rehearsal, she said to me, "I can't do this. I can't lug a baby in the rain just to sit there and do nothing." I couldn't believe it. I was like, "You don't even know him that well. You gonna let this baby come between us?"

Two sides of my brain were firing at the same time. On the surface, I knew it made sense for Melissa not to drag a baby in a car seat in the rain to a rehearsal where she had nothing to do. But deep down inside, in a place that I wasn't fully aware of until years later, her decision to stop coming to those things made me feel like I was no longer a priority. I felt like I came in last place in terms of Melissa's attention.

Obviously, I always wanted kids, but the practical application of my getting less time with my wife was a side effect I hadn't foreseen. I wanted her with me, but I wasn't dumb enough to suggest I wanted her bringing my baby son out in Washington's cold, pitch-black rain for no good reason. In my eyes, she didn't support me the way she used to, and it changed the dynamic of our relationship. The plays I was working on turned into a venture we called The Playmakers, a partnership with my brother and my friend Anthony Davis. In The Playmakers, I was the only one doing stand-up, so that ultimately led to KevOnStage and my YouTube channel. It led to a lot of change, both in my marriage and in my career. And the most important person in my life wasn't involved in it.

None of this changed how much I loved my wife; it just compartmentalized my marriage and my work into two different buckets. Melissa, in my mind, was no longer part of the dream in the same way. But the work needed to be done, so I put my head down and did what I had to do.

Melissa:

When two people have a baby, the hope is that it solidifies them as a couple with a common interest and shared passion. For Kevin and me, despite the fact that we did a great job of sharing the parenting responsibilities, having a baby sent us in opposite directions when it came to the other roles we played in our lives. It was all so subtle that we didn't acknowledge or deal with that reality.

Unspoken resentment was ricocheting back and forth between us. Kevin resented that I couldn't come to all the rehearsals and performances. But I was working eight-hour days, picking up the baby at daycare after work, and returning home to cook dinner. The baby needed to sleep, and nine times out of ten, it was raining outside. Sitting at those rehearsals no longer made sense for my life. I resented that Kevin still had the time and flexibility for the extracurriculars, like his plays and their rehearsals. He played bass in the church band and played basketball and video games with friends. Meanwhile, I'd cut out everything outside work and the baby. I felt like our relationship was shifting into the traditional, stereotypical roles of mommy and daddy.

As a young woman, I pictured in my head who I would be as a grown-up. I wanted to be a lawyer and imagined myself in pencil skirts, blazers, and four-inch heels. I envisioned a powerful woman who carried a briefcase. But after having Isaiah, I was not, in any way, living up to that portrait in my head. On maternity leave, I had postpartum depression, my parents were getting divorced, and I almost had a nervous breakdown. I felt conflicted about going back to work, which completely contradicted how I self-identified. I kept asking myself, *Who am I now?* I didn't recognize myself. I didn't know how I fit in the world under these new circumstances. I was struggling with all of that, and to make matters worse, I didn't discuss any of it with Kev.

My new hazy identity made me insecure. I thought I had to be the responsible one, hold a regular job, keep our health insurance, pay our mortgage. Kevin was out there chasing frivolous dreams that (as far as I was concerned) might never come to pass. I had to be the safety net for our family, and my having to show up at work in the morning provided another reason that I couldn't go with him to clubs to watch him perform.

When Kev felt I wasn't supporting his dreams the way I previously had, he found other people who would—a stage manager and a tour manager who took on the work I used to do for him. And though we didn't realize we were making all these choices at the time, we were creating a new pattern. I no longer was stage manager, so there wasn't a reason to go over blocking, rehearsal times, and auditions. And since I wasn't going to be at his stand-up shows, he didn't really go over jokes with me. When he started on YouTube, he just kind of did his own thing on his channel and shared the successes but not the process. Then Isaiah booked *The Little Rascals* and Kevin went down to L.A. for the shoot and didn't give me daily updates.

As a result, I felt that he no longer wanted my opinion, that I was of no value to him in that part of his life. The divide between us grew wider over the next eleven or twelve years. Essentially, it was an inverse relationship between his career and our connection: As the KevOnStage brand grew, our communication lessened proportionally. With so many balls in the air—my job, our marriage, our kids, Kev's blossoming comedy career—we made decisions for practical purposes, not realizing we'd chosen things that put distance between us.

As I sit writing about this season in our marriage, I can connect dots much more clearly than I could at the time. The birth of a first child marks the end of the era when it's just you and your partner. Now you are parents, you are a family, you are a household with children, and that lasts until the empty nest. It's natural to spend so much time and energy preparing for the baby—getting gear, setting up the nursery, reading about how to care for an infant—that you don't prepare your relationship for the change.

Our communication around Kev's career was lacking. We could have, and should have, been more deliberate about taking the journey together, about dreaming together and celebrating the wins. But instead, we often allowed things to go unsaid and unchecked. Deep down, I think I believed that if I didn't articulate the problems, maybe they wouldn't exist. I could keep the peace, and eventually all would be well.

This avoidance never works. The longer issues go unsaid, the more entrenched they become in your relationship. We both created a narrative about the way our relationship worked, and then each of us operated based on those assumptions. This cycle is dangerous territory for any relationship.

Have you ever been driving and suddenly realized you don't even know how you arrived at your destination? You were just on autopilot? I suspect that a lot of people whose marriages end in divorce ask themselves that question: *How did we get here?*

Kevin:

When the boys were two and four years old, I got fired from my day job. I was devastated, even though I knew it was coming.

There was a festival happening in Seattle, and I was performing there with The Playmakers. The problem was, it took place in the middle of the workday. To get out of the office, I asked my boss if I could go to the festival to try to open some new checking accounts. He was thrilled. To make it all look legit, I gathered the appropriate paperwork, forms, and starter checkbooks on the way out.

Most of the time—and when I say that, I mean 99.9 percent of the time—when you go to events to try to open new accounts, nobody signs up. You end up talking to people and passing out flyers and coming back with nothing. But I wanted to play hooky again when the next performance came up, so I returned to the office and told my boss I had three new accounts from my time at the festival. I counted on the fact that no one would check up on that.

I guess my boss was suspicious, because he told me to fund the accounts and provide the drivers' licenses and signature cards for them. Thus began the hardest I ever worked at that job, trying to open three accounts from two family members and a friend. In the end, there was no faking it. I had just warmed up two chicken thighs in the office microwave when my manager came in and said, "Can I talk to you?" They fired me before I could even take one bite.

Getting fired was the worst rejection I had ever experienced. I had gotten kicked out of ROTC in college, but I didn't care because I hated ROTC. This was different. I felt like a loser, like I was letting my family down. I looked like one of those no-good men in movies where the wife makes all the money and the husband can't hold down a job.

I told Melissa that I didn't want to file for unemployment because it felt like a handout, but she wasn't going for it. We needed the money. When I went to the unemployment office, I had to take the boys with me. I held both of their hands crossing the street and asked for government assistance with both of them watching. When I got home, I had to assume domestic responsibilities like cooking and cleaning and taking care of the boys. One morning I made Melissa's lunch, and she gave my forehead a kiss as she headed out the door for work. It killed me. I felt like Melissa was Don Draper and I was Betty. The only time I felt confident was when I went out to do the comedy stuff at night.

By the time the first tour came around in 2018, things were looking up as far as my career. I made more money in one month than either of us had been making in a year. Melissa's safety-net thinking was no longer necessary. But when we talked about the tour and I would ask her to quit her job and work full-time with me, she wouldn't do it. I couldn't believe it. *Not only does she not believe in me, but she doesn't want to go back to a time when we did all that stuff together. She wants to do her own thing.* In my mind, this was our chance to be together again—to go back to the way things used to be. Her not wanting to devote her career to the tour meant that she didn't support me, didn't want to be together on that path, so from then on, I stopped sharing information and details with her that related to my career.

Melissa:

Wait! Wait! Let me explain! As I mentioned earlier, we all create narratives that become the scripts for our relationship. The story we tell ourselves about our marriage determines what we believe, how we act, and how we respond to new challenges. In the story I'd always told myself, I was a hardworking, successful woman living a very practical, nine-to-five life.

As a child, I watched my parents struggle to make ends meet. I remember constant discussions about bills and whether or when they could be paid, which taught me that money is limited and finite. That backstory, coupled with Kevin having been fired from his job, made me even more entrenched in the role I'd taken in this family: responsible breadwinner. We had kids and bills, and I made sure I was the last line of defense. When Kev first asked me to walk away from my job, I couldn't do it, because that's not how I was written. And of course Kevin took that personally, seeing it as an indictment of his ability to provide, because that's how *he* was written.

Ten months after the tour started, I left my stable job, imagining that a glorious partnership would bloom between Kevin and me. I wanted to be fully immersed in KevOnStage, but I still found myself on the outside. I was used to having a clear job description that stated what was required of me on a daily basis. Entrepreneurship is the exact opposite: I had no idea what my day-to-day life was going to look like, and now there was the added stress of travel and not having time to really talk outside work.

I thought I would quit my job, go on tour with Kevin, and the underlying issues we'd been having since Isaiah was born twelve years prior would melt away. It's kind of like when a couple tries to fix their marriage by having a baby. The hope is that the excitement of something new and wonderful will make them stronger as husband and wife. For us, the tour was that baby. We thought it would infuse our marriage with newness and fun and togetherness, but it was really just a distraction from what was really going on. Not surprisingly, nothing was fixed. Now that we were working together, we were constantly in each other's faces. Avoidance was no longer an option.

One day, we were both supposed to have a work call with Kevin's tour manager. I was home with the boys and Kevin was in the car. I kept waiting for the call to come in, but it never did. When Kevin got home, I asked him why the conference call was canceled. He told me he just took it alone, since he figured I was busy making dinner and helping with homework. It made me feel like I was on the outside looking in. It got to the point where I figured I should go back to work, because things were better between us when we didn't spend the days together, when we were both doing our own thing.

It all came back to those roles we'd been acting out unconsciously. Kev and I were in a new season of life. Our circumstances had changed, and it was time to audition for new parts. Instead, we stayed cast in our previous roles, which no longer served us. We were still holding on to an arrangement that served us well when Kevin got fired and I thought of myself as the safety net. Both of us felt that dynamic, but we didn't articulate it—not inwardly and not to each other. The resulting issues simmered under the surface for way too long.

Kevin:

Years later, I have come to realize that my "with me or against me" philosophy played a role in the problems that arose between me and Melissa. I'm not proud of it, but this philosophy stems from my relationship (or lack thereof) with my birth father and the fact that my brother and sister had godparents but I did not. My real dad gave up on me without even trying. Sports were my life, and all of my teammates' parents seemed to find a way to be at the games, particularly at the home games. But my dad, and even my mother, hardly ever came.

When you're playing basketball and you hit a three, you want to look into the stands and see your parents' reactions. One time, after a home game where I'd played really well, I walked into my house and found my mom, my grandma, and my aunt watching *Wheel of Fortune*. It hit me hard that they were all together, sitting around watching TV, when they could have easily been at my game.

I'm not angry with my parents, but all of that did shape my perspective of what it means to have people in my life who support me and what that is supposed to look like. When Melissa stopped coming to my rehearsals—and later, didn't quit her job to work full-time with me—she became, in my head, another family member who was unwilling to support me. And for years, I was completely unaware that I had cast her in that role.

Melissa and I have never had the big hurdles that often undo a marriage—infidelity, abuse, financial worries—where it's obvious changes have to be made. But the less obvious issues are often equally detrimental. Instead of fighting about our expectations and changing roles, we got quieter. Instead of blaming and finger-pointing, we ignored the problems. It all took place on a subconscious level, but feeling like you're not together, like you're not aligned, is dangerous. If that kind of fissure goes untreated, it can do real damage to your marriage.

In the midst of this second round of the tour, when Melissa was with me full-time, the kids had a soccer game coming up. Melissa mentioned she was going to buy something for Isaiah's uniform, and I casually mentioned where she might be able to get the item more easily and inexpensively. She snapped. "I'm good at my job!" she said. I was like, "Huh?" And she went on, "People respect me at my job." I wasn't even talking about her job. The subtext was that she felt like I didn't respect the work she did. Other people supported her and didn't question her, and she wanted the same from me. At the time, I didn't catch it. And of course I didn't—I wasn't looking for it.

That was the moment I realized we needed help. That kind of disconnect was out of range for us. We could not fix this problem on our own with the communication tactics we had at our disposal. It was time to get outside help in the form of a couples therapist. We just didn't have the tools to get beyond the same negative cycle we were repeating.

I think I took a little pride in the fact that we hadn't been to therapy. We were high school sweethearts; we never outwardly argued; we were faithful; we were solid! I thought of us as being stronger than couples who went to therapy: *Look at us, better than y'all!* And if I'm being honest, part of me worried that going to therapy meant we were broken beyond repair. But it came to a point where it was time to make a choice: keep up the pride of no therapy or fix the problem. We chose to fix the problem.

Melissa:

As we have said, marriage has phases. And your relationship—how you view and treat each other—will go through changes as these phases come and go. Having kids was the first indication that even though Kev and I were taking on life's challenges together, we weren't living every aspect of our lives with each other like we had previously.

Two life-changing events helped us identify these issues and get to work remedying them. The first was my quitting my job and joining Kevin in his journey as a performer. The second was the pandemic. (We'll share more on that in chapter 9, "Quarantine Be Hard.") Those were the two seismic shifts that exposed the holes in our foundation. Today, fifteen years after we became parents, the changes and issues that first came up when we had Isaiah are being resolved. We work to have honest conversations so unresolved feelings don't linger for as long as they previously have. As we take on new challenges, both personally and professionally, and as our roles change with each venture, we consciously discuss the emotions those changes are producing. It's a really important function of the relationship check-ins.

Kevin:

We have a full-blown teenager, and yet we continue to repair the damage that arose when he was born. We're still in the healing process. We've stopped the bleeding, but even now, we aren't working together smoothly like we did when we first started out. I have faith in us, though. We'll get there.

Relationship Check-In

As the seasons of your marriage change, so do the hats you wear. We suggest you and your partner check in with each other about the roles you play in your relationship. Ask each other these questions:

- How would you identify yourself and the roles you play in your relationship?
- Are you satisfied with those roles?
- How do you view your partner's roles?
- Do your roles complement your partner's roles?
- Do your roles conflict with or contradict your partner's roles?
- Would you accept a shift or change in the role(s) your partner takes on?
- Are you willing to adjust your role(s) to suit your partner's desire?

Chapter Six

Fidelity Be Hard

When a man and woman get married, they make some version of the promise that they will "forsake all others." Even if the words are not specifically articulated, fidelity is typically assumed in the taking of those vows. However, statistics tell us that we can't rely on these vows to ensure faithfulness in our marriage. The pledge of monogamy is front and center in the oath we take as husband and wife, and yet affairs, in one form or another, seem to be happening in every corner of the globe. The sad thing is that the two of us learned firsthand about infidelity's impact on a marriage through a couple close to us: Melissa's parents. They are our reference point for many of the lessons we've learned about cheating.

As we witnessed, even the relationships that seem most solid can be vulnerable to broken vows. While most people will say cheating is wrong, infidelity is more common than we'd like to admit. We have said it before and will say it again: Marriage be hard. It's only normal for the bloom to fall off the rose as couples grow comfortable and sometimes complacent. Some people get restless. Some people get careless. Some feel taken for granted and underappreciated. Oftentimes cheating is less about wanting a new relationship and more about wanting the current relationship to be different.

Our advice, which we'll unpack in this chapter, is twofold:

1. Protect your marriage from the threat of infidelity.
2. If you think you could never forgive a cheating spouse, we advise, "Never say never!"

Kevin:

Many people think that since Liss and I got together in high school, marriage must have been easier for us than for those who met later in life. Person after person has said how simple it must be for me and Liss to stay faithful and true because we've essentially been together forever. In my experience, it's the opposite. The longer you've been married, the more susceptible you are to infidelity if you aren't actively working to keep things fresh. Familiarity breeds contempt in all walks of life. A routine can be useful and comfortable for a while, but soon you're stuck in a rut and feeling bored. For me and Melissa, the pandemic was a huge routine disruption that helped recalibrate us in a good way. (More on that in chapter 9, "Quarantine Be Hard.")

When you meet and commit at seventeen years old, you've got a lot of changing and growing ahead of you, and there's no guarantee that the two of you are going to change and grow in a way that maintains your compatibility. When people meet later in life, after they're fully formed adults, there will be fewer surprises—what you see is what you get. Either way, if you want to keep your marriage healthy, you have to do the personal work as you grow, change, and evolve.

Affairs, whether they are physical or emotional, are usually a symptom that something else in your marriage isn't working. They happen when a person isn't getting what they need from their spouse. The new person is often filling that vacancy. A man might cheat with a woman who makes him feel powerful when his wife does not. Maybe the new person speaks your love language in a way your partner isn't up for. Either way, it's not your partner's fault if you've kept them in the dark. Your spouse might not ever know that your feelings and needs aren't being met. It's up to you to tell them.

Melissa:

I know it's totally on brand for me to say that it all comes down to communication, trust, and having a voice. But it needs to be said. You need to be your true, authentic, transparent, vulnerable self with your partner. Unspoken needs are one of the most direct paths to disappointment, and a lack of communication could be how you lose your spouse. It's common to romanticize the relationship you're in: *If we're in love, if we're married, if you're my partner and we're meant to be, you should automatically understand and know what my needs are.* That's just not true. As we've said, the "you should know" approach is a danger like no other. You have to speak up, and you have to do it early and often.

By maintaining communication, you protect your marriage. Just as the White House has security on duty at all times, not exclusively in instances of imminent danger, you must place that same value on your relationship and maintain those safeguards. Many people, as time goes by, find that the novelty of the relationship wears off. When that happens and you feel comfortable with your spouse, it's not uncommon to get a little lazy. Maybe you stop making all the effort you made at the beginning. Maybe you stop flirting, stop complimenting your partner, stop looking at each other with googly eyes. You might not even realize you're missing those things until someone else offers them up. You don't have to be looking for it to bump into someone who reminds you how good it feels to get all that stuff you used to get from your spouse. That's why we suggest making an effort to safeguard your relationship from that kind of danger. Your relationship is precious and needs to be protected.

I used to feel very strongly that an affair would be the end of my relationship. In fact, I said to Kev before we got married, "If you cheat, I'm gone." After investing years in our relationship and speaking to therapists and marriage counselors, I have changed my tune. Now, I believe that marriage can survive infidelity. Esther Perel talks about how an affair can lead to the rebirth of a relationship; it can provide the opportunity to analyze what's working, what's missing, and what needs to be changed in your relationship. The reborn relationship has potential to be filled with honesty and more intimacy than ever before. There might even be more vigor and intentionality than there was prior to the affair.[1]

Kevin:

Our relationship has evolved over many seasons of life. First, we had high school love, which was totally pure, no complications, no kids, no bills, no jobs. Obviously, we can never go back to that season. As the wise elder Slim Charles once said to Bodie on a Baltimore corner, "The thing about the old days— they the old days."[2] You need to focus on what is happening now.

In the current season of our marriage, as Melissa and I talked through the topics we've written about in this book, we had an honest conversation about what might tempt us to cheat. Melissa said that her weakness would be a man who was vulnerable and made her feel *seen* all the time. I told her that my weakness would be a woman who was verbally affirming and very forward sexually. My vulnerability lies in feeling desired.

Truth be told, it was a very difficult conversation to have. But very, very necessary. Now we know, even more clearly, what needs to be shored up. We are working to fulfill those needs for each other so that someone else offering them won't be tempting to either of us. If you're reading this, thinking, *Now, here's my opportunity to slide in some DMs and shoot my shot,* I'm sorry. It's too late. Those areas have already been reinforced. Plus, we wrote this book at minimum a year before you are reading it, so imagine how much stronger we are by now. You missed your chance, you evil little home-wrecker, you.

Emotional Affairs

Not all affairs are alike, but they all involve some form of secret keeping. And they don't necessarily have to be physical. An emotional affair, while not overtly sexual, can be just as damaging to your marriage as a sexual one. It may seem harmless because the physical line has not been crossed (at least not yet), but it is still an affair. If there are secrets and dishonesty, it's an affair.

You might be wondering, *What qualifies as an emotional affair? At what point do talking, flirting, texting, and conversations on social media become evidence of one?* We think it's pretty easy to determine whether you're engaged in an emotional affair. Ask yourself these questions:

1. Is your spouse unaware that you're communicating with this person?
2. Are you hiding the content of the communication?
3. Would you be ashamed or afraid to admit to your partner how frequently you and the other person communicate?

If you can answer yes to any of these questions, an affair is going on. Put it this way: If, in explaining the relationship to your spouse, you put the word *just* in front of the words *a friend,* there's a problem. And when you're having more conversations than necessary and appropriate with another person—a person you are attracted to—it can come at the expense of your marriage relationship. You end up talking to, confiding in, and trusting that person more than you do your spouse. Even if there is nothing physical going on, it's the kind of attention you should be giving to your partner.

Melissa:

It's important to make the distinction between flirting and an emotional affair. Flirting, while not necessarily right, is just flirting. If flirting is not discriminatory—if you or your spouse flirts with a wide range of friends and acquaintances—it's usually harmless. Some people know all too well that they're married to a flirt. Side note: If your flirting is in any way disrespectful to your spouse, then you better knock that off. However, flirting is not nearly as dangerous as an emotional affair. Your relationship is in peril once there is real emotional intimacy with someone outside your marriage.

Kevin:

Emotional affairs have gotten much easier and more pervasive since social media entered our lives. Too many people use social media to overshare about their lives and inappropriately connect with others, and as a result, social media can be dangerous for your relationship. First of all, social media is a time sucker that takes quality minutes—and probably hours—away from your marriage. Second, it's telling how often social media (and Facebook specifically) is cited as evidence of infidelity. People used to have to go on business trips or to their high school reunions to connect with people, to behave in a way that they wouldn't if their spouses were present. But now they can go on social media and have that experience.

Recently, I was reminded of how social media can lead to problems when I was on the road and encountering European-style showers right here in the US. Let me paint the picture for you: These showers have no curtain, no door, and a glass panel that for some reason covers only about half the shower. I was going from hotel to hotel, navigating these half walls of glass, spraying water everywhere, and barely getting clean, so I decided to do a Snapchat series about how much I hate those showers. I brought the phone into the bathroom with me and made a funny post.

Later that day, a woman commented, "Ooh, I was looking in the mirror trying to see something." I immediately blocked her. But I was well aware that if my ego went unchecked, a comment like that could turn into a dangerous scenario. This woman was pressing on one of those weaknesses I mentioned earlier. My wife is very conservative in the bedroom. This woman, based on her message, was clearly much more forward. That's the kind of situation that can be problematic. If I hadn't blocked her, innocent conversations could have blurred into not-so-innocent conversations.

Infidelity never starts off as infidelity. You can be at work talking about data reports, and the next thing you know, you done fell in some coochie. In the same way, emotional affairs, whether over social media or at work, never start with someone asking, "Hey, do you want to cheat on your wife?" They start with little comments, sexy suggestions, flirting that seems harmless at first. That door can open at any time if someone chooses to engage.

To clarify, we cannot blame adultery on Facebook. Obviously, cheating existed long before social media, and in many cases, people who want to have affairs will find a way to make it happen. But even though we can't condemn social media as the root cause of infidelity, we can say that social media is providing new and easy opportunities for people to connect. We know a man and a woman who had known each other for a while and were both married to other people when they connected on Facebook. The Facebook messaging turned into an affair and resulted in two divorces.

Think about it. There's someone you used to date or used to crush on. You don't know their number or their email address, but you can probably find them on Facebook, and when you do, maybe those old feelings start rushing back. Also, when you connect with someone you knew when you were young, you might feel young again just by talking to that person. You might even still see each other the way you did way back then.

Melissa:

If you think your social media activity should be private, we disagree. We say share your passwords to your social media accounts with your spouse. Knowing that your partner has your passwords is a step toward protecting your relationship. Think about it this way: You share a bed, a mortgage, and a car payment with this person. Why not passwords? Why should texts, emails, and direct messages be private when you have a joint checking account and know each other's bodies inside and out? The key is to have nothing to hide. If you consider keeping your passwords (and thus your social media activity) part of your entitled privacy, your partner would be justified in wondering if you've got something to hide.

Some might make the argument, "If you trust me, I shouldn't have to share my passwords." That's when I like to pull out the phrase *trust but verify*. Privacy is not a valid argument if you and your spouse are on life's journey together. It's hard to trust a person who wants to keep passwords private.

You might be asking, "If we have each other's passwords, does that mean we should be able to go snooping through our partner's social media activity?" Let us put that question to bed right now. Sharing should not lead to snooping. Snooping is a symptom of a much bigger issue. If you're snooping, you're probably doing so out of insecurity or a lack of trust. Get to the bottom of why you might be snooping, and deal with that. If you're suspicious, you might need to investigate why you're feeling that way. A conversation is much more productive than snooping.

Kevin:

It's wise to limit the personal messages you send on social media. If you message someone, keep it brief so it doesn't bleed into something inappropriate or misleading. Don't make the mistake of venting about your marriage or becoming a shoulder for someone else to cry on. That shoulder can easily become a different body part to find comfort in.

It should be stated that emotional affairs happen in all sorts of other settings. They start in person all the time, very often at work. After all, we often spend more hours in a day with our colleagues than with our partners. Also, people usually look pretty good at work. They tend to dress nice, they have their hair done, and they've got themselves all put together. When you work with someone, you don't see that person get frustrated with their kids, burn dinner, or put on their threadbare comfy sweatpants. At home, you see your partner in his or her full humanity, and it's not always glorious.

The scenario we discuss in the "Jealousy Be Hard" chapter— the one where the woman I had a crush on in high school baked me a birthday cake and sent texts that Melissa flagged as dangerously inappropriate—was absolutely the beginning of an emotional affair. I might call it a baby emotional affair. If Melissa hadn't put an end to it, that baby emotional affair might have matured into a toddler or maybe a full-grown adult.

All this talk about dangerous communication with someone, whether at work or via social media, might make you wonder, *Can you have friends of the opposite sex?* Let us start by saying that all relationships—marriages and friendships outside marriage—are different. We suggest you ask yourself, *If I weren't married, would I be interested in this person sexually?* If the answer is yes, you cannot hang out. You need to be honest with yourself and accountable to yourself. If you can admit that you're attracted to the other person—that if you were alone, you're not sure what might happen—then you need to make sure you're never alone with that person. That can be tricky, particularly if we're talking about people at work. Naturally, you can't get someone fired just because they're attractive.

Again, be accountable. Unchecked, an emotional affair could lead to a physical affair.

Melissa:

Tapping the mic

Is this thing on? Now listen, I totally get why Kevin would describe that relationship with the actress and amateur baker as a *baby* emotional affair, but I'm here to tell you—it was bigger than a baby. It may not have been fully grown, but looking back on it with what I know now, I believe it was a blossoming and growing emotional affair.

Keep in mind, our marriage was in a season of transition: I was a new mom, I had retired as Kev's stage manager and had stopped going to his rehearsals, and my parents were getting divorced. Transitions are some of the most fragile times in a relationship. (That's why a peaceful transition of power is a central tenet of American democracy, because chaos puts the security of the nation at risk.) The truth is, our marriage was extremely vulnerable during that time. We were new parents, and we were moving into different roles, figuring out how to go from a childless couple to a family. Looking back, it's by the grace of God that Kev's emotional affair with this woman didn't turn into a physical affair. At the time, I was unaware of how vulnerable we actually were.

Today, I try to be more sensitive to seasons of transition. I make an effort to recognize when Kevin and I are on different emotional planes with whatever is going on in our lives. I tend to be more emotionally fragile and sensitive, while Kevin mostly just charges ahead. When we are on opposite ends like that, it shows up as emotional turmoil in our relationship. We need to be more open with our partners about these things.

When Kevin started touring, we knew we were going to be seeing less and less of each other, so we implemented weekly date nights. Later, in therapy, we realized that a date once a week wasn't enough. We needed to be more deliberate about staying connected while Kevin was gone. I didn't want to bother Kevin when he was on the road because it seemed like he was having great fun. Turns out, Kevin was thinking the same thing about me. It looked to him like I was having fun at home with my sister and friend, so he didn't want to bother me. But during this season of transition, we needed to connect more often in an effort to protect our relationship. I told Kev I needed connection and specifically asked him to check in. That allowed him to share his feelings with me. He started calling me in the morning, in the afternoon, and at night after the show. We actually spoke over the phone instead of trading a couple texts throughout the weekend. He made that effort to protect our marriage.

It's worth reiterating: You do not have to protect friendships, but it is crucial—and one of your main responsibilities—to protect your marriage. If someone, perhaps a person you consider a friend, is sending you messages that you're not sharing with your spouse, engaging in behavior with you that is the beginning of an emotional affair, you must remember, that person is not to blame. *You* took the vows. It is *your* job to keep that marriage intact. Likewise, if your spouse is talking too much to someone else or the content of their communication is inappropriate, don't go pointing fingers at the other woman or man. It is *your* woman or man who entered into the marriage contract. You and your spouse have only each other to answer to.

Healing the Hurt

Melissa:

If infidelity has impacted your relationship, there are steps to take to recover. It's not easy, but it's possible. First you have to grieve the loss of what *was* so you can accept what actually *is*. We all enter relationships with ideas of what they could be, and when they don't turn out that way, we must grieve. Grieving looks different for everyone, but it usually starts with acknowledging the loss. You need to indulge in your sadness without judging yourself or thinking you were naïve. In cases of a cheating spouse, grieving will likely come with anger, because infidelity makes a person feel duped. No one likes to feel stupid. That's where the vulnerability comes into play.

I will never be the person to recommend whether a person should stay or leave after there has been infidelity. I will say, however, that if you decide to stay, you need to recognize that rebuilding your relationship is not a linear process. As we learned from Esther Perel, the rebuilding will not incrementally, day by day, get better and easier. Some days you and your partner will feel united and close and everything will be going smoothly. Then a trigger—an intrusive thought, a movie, a commercial, a word, a color—might remind you that your partner strayed, and that trigger can be a setback. You have to work through it and recognize it's all part of the process.

When a person who was cheated on decides to leave the marriage, they're often met with celebration and pats on the back from people close to them. "Good for you," they will hear. But I feel very strongly that we should not judge the person who decides to stay. As Esther Perel notes, staying requires a lot of work—more work than anyone who has never been in that situation could ever imagine.[3] Just as I never judge people who stay, though, I never judge people who leave, because there are often valid reasons for leaving. It takes two people to be fully invested in a marriage, and if one person is not willing to put in the work, if they're not going to change, if they're not going to show up, it might be time to go.

My friend cheated on her husband, and as they repaired their relationship, he had to work hard to respect her privacy despite his instincts to snoop into all her personal business. Even though he was the innocent party, he had to do all the heavy lifting when it came to rebuilding the trust. If you choose to stay, you have to fight the urge to go looking for trouble, to let mistrust guide you.

Just like the world will never be the same after 9/11 or after the pandemic, your marriage will not be the same after infidelity. And just like we don't want to go back to a pre-9/11 world where we were unaware of the dangers, we don't want to go back to a relationship before the infidelity was discovered. You can romanticize what the relationship was, but in reality, that relationship was broken.

While many applaud the person who was cheated on for walking away from the marriage, others encourage that person to fight for their marriage. In my opinion, that is an unfair burden to place on someone who didn't mess up. *So, let me get this straight. I didn't commit a sin, I didn't step out on my husband, I was true, but I am the one who needs to do all the heavy lifting?* It's up to *both* people in the marriage to get to the root of the problems that led to the affair.

If you do decide to stay, here is my list of things to consider:

1. It might go without saying, but the cheating has to stop. Everything about the relationship between the cheating

spouse and the outside person needs to end. Those relational ties have to be completely severed.

2. Find the underlying reason the affair took place. Cheating shines a light on the fact that parts of your relationship are broken. Darkness can't live in light. Agreeing to stay in the marriage allows you both to work on those parts. Keep in mind, though, that you should not need to go through infidelity to deal with repairing those aspects of your relationship.

    Inevitably, the person who gets cheated on is going to ask the cheating spouse, "Why?" Cheating forces the conversation. Chances are, both people were aware of the problems but no one talked about them until the infidelity was discovered. It becomes time to have the conversation that should have happened before the cheating took place. And that conversation should take place in the presence of a licensed professional.

3. Find a mediator or therapist. A third party can be very helpful in interpreting and helping you and your partner articulate your feelings and needs—and, when necessary, provide a new perspective.

4. The trust has to be rebuilt, and that will take time. As discussed above, the recovery isn't linear.

Relationship Check-In

Our relationship check-in for this chapter is all about protecting your marriage from potential infidelity. Ask yourself and your partner these questions:

- Do you have unspoken needs that aren't being met?
- Are you communicating your needs to your partner?
- Are you listening and paying attention to your spouse's needs?
- Are you and/or your spouse transitioning into a new season of life? If so, are you checking in on how their needs might be changing as a result of what you're going through?

Chapter Seven

Fighting Be Hard

They say the only two certainties in life are death and taxes. In marriage, there's another certainty: fighting. Even if you and your partner make every effort to do right to and for each other, you're going to fight. Fighting is a part of marriage that we don't really discuss when we plan our lives together. We talk about how many kids we want, what holidays we'll celebrate, and where we want to go on vacation, but we don't prepare to fight fairly.

Fighting is natural. It's a way to remember that you're two different people with different ideas, worldviews, and priorities. But for years, we were so dedicated to presenting a united front that we didn't work out our differences. Even as we write this book, we struggle with closing the loop on disagreements. We have come to realize that the two of us are equally bad at fighting but in different ways. And not even in ways that complement each other.

Early on, the problem was that we didn't fight at all. We didn't talk openly about our beefs, which meant there were things (a lot of things) we just weren't dealing with at all. We

didn't call each other names or do all those dangerous and abu-
sive things that people think of when they think of unhealthy
fighting, but that didn't mean we were dealing with conflict in
a healthy way. Even people who fight unfairly benefit from voicing their honest opinions, which we failed to do.

Arguments can be productive, and you can learn from them
if you fight fair. For us, learning to fight fair has led to reconciliation and ultimately getting our relationship needs met.

Melissa:

My parents did not fight fair. Over the course of their marriage,
they had two fighting gears: full throttle and total silence. When
we were young, my sisters and I had front-row seats to all the
craziness: throwing things, yelling, the whole nine yards. Not at
all what I now know to be fighting fair.

After my dad got saved, there was a complete, 180-degree
shift in their marriage. In my mind, it made perfect sense: Jesus
came in and fixed it. Because I didn't see them argue anymore,
I assumed their relationship was now flawless, but really, it was
just a lot of silence. My ignorant takeaway was that a good
marriage, one that is touched by Jesus, is one with no disagreements. And that's what I came to expect when Kev and I got
married. In fact, I might even say I was afraid of fighting because I had seen how bad it could get. That's how I adopted my
go-to tactic of shutting down.

For me and Kevin, fighting out loud is not the issue. What
we do is fight in silence, which ultimately starts an internal war.
I'm not a name caller, a yeller, a blamer, a scorekeeper, or a
fusser. Those aren't my methods of fighting unfairly. When I'm
triggered, I shut down—meaning everything about my body
language suggests I am not open for business. I isolate myself

by turning away, getting completely quiet. I put a force field around myself that communicates loud and clear, "Leave me alone."

I have since learned that staying silent to keep the peace is actually a trauma response. The self-work for me that came with learning to fight fair was recognizing my triggers and working through them to keep Kev from stepping on them.

I like to say I have three primary triggers that bring on my shutdown mode:

1. Being overlooked
2. Being overlooked
3. Being overlooked

It surfaces in many different ways, and not just with Kevin. It grinds my gears if I feel I'm being ignored, if my ideas are dismissed, or if my suggestions go unaddressed. Let me make something clear here: I do not need to be praised or complimented, only to be acknowledged as a person in the room. I have learned to talk about the need to feel and be heard. Kevin has learned to talk about his need to be affirmed. It's not easy, but we're getting there.

At the end of the day, it comes down to this: What you think, feel, see, or assume creates a reality. If I believe that Kevin is constantly overlooking me, I will interpret everything he says and does through that lens. It's like being in a court of law. You make a case and arrange the evidence to support your theory. You can even position your witness to give testimony that supports your view of the matter. "Judge, add the last comment to the list of evidence!" That way of thinking and framing your partner's words does not give them the benefit of the doubt.

Kevin:

The only time I saw a glimpse of her mother's temper in Melissa was the story we shared in the jealousy chapter, when the woman I knew from high school got inappropriate with the birthday cake. That was when I realized Melissa had that fiery temper. I had no idea it lurked in her until then, and I knew I never wanted to make her that angry again. I mean, she threw a BlackBerry. She was domestic-violencing me! Do you know how heavy BlackBerrys were? Luckily I'm a finely tuned athletic machine and was able to juke that thing when it sailed my way. Otherwise, there's no telling what would have happened.

Like Melissa, I learned about fighting from my parents. But my parents fought fairly. No yelling, no violence, no pettiness, no name calling. They kept the main thing the main thing. But I do have a grainy picture in my head of a time before my dad came into our lives. My mom was with one of her boyfriends, a guy who always yelled. *Always*. She was scared all the time. I remember once when he asked for a sandwich and she made him a scrambled-egg sandwich. He yelled at the top of his lungs, "I don't want no egg sandwich!"; then he smashed the plate with his fist. The food went flying, and the dish split into pieces. My brother grabbed me by the arm and ushered me outside, where we took a long walk in the pouring rain. I sloshed around thinking, *I hope my mom is okay*. I had never seen her look so scared. That's my last memory of that boyfriend. And my last memory of her being mistreated.

When I was six years old, my stepdad came into our lives. He is, for all intents and purposes, my father and the man I call Dad. He always had a calm voice when he spoke to anyone, especially my mom. He was soft and soothing with her: "Sheila, what would you like? How can I help? Okay, I didn't know you meant it like that. Yes, I understand. I'll take care of it." I noticed that he made sacrifices for her and for us.

Like Melissa, my instincts are not to yell or name call or be petty. Those are all things that hinder couples from getting to the root of their issues. But I too have been guilty of going too far to avoid conflict. I think early in our relationship, the reason I didn't want to fight was the perception among our friends and family that went something like this: "Oh, Kevin and Melissa, you're so cute and perfect. You're so in love. You never argue. I want a relationship just like yours."

It felt important for me to be able to say that these friends were right, that we never argued, that we were always happy. If given the choice to either contradict what everyone thought and be honest with Melissa about my feelings or keep the fairy tale alive, I would have chosen maintaining the fairy tale. Of course, I could have just lied to people and said everything was great even if it wasn't, but I thought I needed to keep it up for real. I thought we needed to be getting along at all times.

Melissa:

There are very specific guidelines that we recommend for fighting fair. But before we jump in, it probably makes sense to tell you about the biggest fight Kev and I ever had. It touches on the guidelines listed below, because we broke several of the rules.

When we were juniors in high school, I was in the driver's seat of my car, and my passengers were Kev and my cousin Tony. We were on our way to a track meet. The two of them were fussing and fighting, being backseat drivers, trying to give me directions and telling me where to park. I was not having it. I told them, "Y'all are sitting in my car. You can either be quiet, willing passengers, or y'all can get out." They kept at it. They would not stop all the noise, trying to tell me what to do and how to do it. Finally, I pulled over in frustration and said, "Both y'all can get out of my car." They got out of the car and walked the rest of the way.

Fast-forward to fourteen years later, we were married and living in Los Angeles, and our friends had flown out to visit us. When we picked them up at the airport, they were starving, but it was late at night and the only options were fast food. So we headed to Jack in the Box, with Kev driving and me directing him.

Before long, Kevin was getting stressed. "Where is it? Where is it? I don't see it." I started to worry that I didn't have the location right. Our two friends were sitting in the back seat. It was late, and we were all hungry and tired.

From there, the tension mounted. I was trying to help Kev find Jack in the Box, but we didn't see it—and I admit, I have a horrible sense of direction. Kevin kept asking where it was and I kept telling him to keep driving, that it was just a little farther down the street. We ended up getting into a tiff about the location of this Jack in the Box. It was such a dumb thing to fight about, but in the moment, it felt so important. I don't recall the last thing I said or what the final straw was, but out of sheer frustration and exasperation, Kevin turned to me and said, "This is my car. If you don't like it, you can get out." I was so mad I could have cried.

A little context for you: This was five years after Kev had been fired from his job as a banker. When he was unemployed, not bringing in a dime to our household, I never made him feel less than. I never pulled that card on him, never talked to him that way—even if I had a right to, since I was bringing in the money. Now, cut to the night of this fight. It was right around the time that Kev's first comedy tour was kicking off. He had just bought that car, and it was in his name. I thought, *Oh, he's gonna go on tour as a comedian. He's feeling himself, and now he's throwing it in my face.* I wanted to scream, "I will not depend on you for nothing. EVER!" Our friends were in the back seat, witnesses to all of it, so I didn't say a word. But Kev's words in the car that night were a *huge* part of the reason I was later reluctant to quit my job. Even though Kev was earning a lot, enough to support me and our family, that fight incentivized me to keep earning my own paycheck.

Here's why Kevin's tirade hit me hard: My dad was raised by a single mom who could barely make ends meet. My dad always told me and my sisters, "Don't depend on nobody for nothing. Ever." He wanted us to be prepared to take care of ourselves in any and all circumstances. He taught us to drive a stick shift, fix a tire, and change our oil, all with the purpose of never needing a man. I remember my dad saying, "In the event that something goes down, you will be prepared and know how to take care of yourself."

Kev's words that night triggered the memory of my dad's warnings. Now that my husband was making more money, he believed he had power over me and would use it against me. It was all about power.

Kevin:

My side of this story is entirely based on two words: *my car.* When Melissa said that in high school, she had a car and I had a bike. I felt so small and powerless. She punked me in front of my boy like that, and I never conveyed to her how small she made me feel. Like, *Dang, she could really punk me like this, and there's nothing I can do about it.* Without even being aware of it, those two words stuck with me all those years. And since we never discussed it, Melissa certainly had no idea of the impact her words had on me.

I knew what I said was wrong. It was condescending, and I'd embarrassed her in front of our friends. That would all be true even if it didn't trigger other feelings in Melissa—but I had no idea the impact my comment made and what it stirred up in her. She took it as a flex, a reminder that I held the power in our relationship.

In the moment, I saw Melissa turn cold, but I had no clue that my words drummed up all that history for her. Her reaction manifested itself as her shutting down, which I translated as, "I won't need you, won't come toward you. I will be distant from you. I won't miss you." So now I'm feeling like my wife does not desire or need me. I had no intention of actually making her get out of the car. I just finally had the chance to say "my car" like she once did. It was petty and competitive. And the funniest part of this story (reminder: comedy is tragedy plus time) is that I didn't realize any of this until we were in the car fighting about Jack in the Box.

When we got home that night, Melissa cried and cried. She told me how embarrassed she'd felt in front of our friends. My words made her feel powerless and unimportant, and she'd never made me feel that way when I got fired. She laid out how and why my words stung so badly. By the next morning, we were no longer fighting, but I could tell it still stung. I knew I messed up. I was trippin' and I had to fix it.

Whether it's about deep-seated issues or thoughtless throw-away comments, you will fight with your partner. It's unavoidable, so we suggest adhering to some guidelines that ensure that those fights don't turn into all-out wars. Let's start with the first rule of fighting fair:

1. Keep the Main Thing the Main Thing

This is first and foremost: When you're arguing about the toilet paper roll, stay focused on the toilet paper roll. Don't bring up a past issue to strengthen your case, especially if it's not relevant. When we assume an "I want to win" strategy, it makes us dig into our arsenal and pull up old arguments and past offenses. That's not fighting fair. We strongly encourage you to let go of crimes committed in the past.

If you have beefed about a similar subject in the past and decided to let it go, you have to stick to letting it go. Don't let days and weeks and months of irritations that you haven't let go of resurface when a new issue arises.

Kevin:

In the Jack in the Box incident, I did not focus on the issue. I was definitely pulling up that old hurt, bringing up a past issue to get back at Melissa. And the Jack in the Box incident isn't the only time I've been guilty of a similar offense. There have been other times when something was bugging me but I let it fester instead of speaking up. I wasn't fully honest with Melissa about how I felt, which led to later arguments when I didn't keep the main thing the main thing.

As I've grown and evolved, I've learned that this story is a perfect example of my need to be affirmed. When Melissa told me to get out of her car in high school, she made me feel like a loser. I guess, for all those years, that lack of affirmation was present beneath the surface and I allowed it to simmer silently. No wonder it came up when we were tired, hungry, and lost.

2. No Name-Calling

Other than it being petty and childish, the real problem with name-calling is that it leaves stains that last longer than the real argument. For example, if you're fighting about how your spouse spends too much money on a pair of shoes and you call your partner stupid and irresponsible, those words are going to linger long after the argument is over and the shoes have gone out of style. The other reason name-calling is outside the boundaries of fighting fair is that it dilutes the real issue at hand. If your partner calls you a lazy, useless fool instead of explaining how and why you didn't get the promotion at work, you'll jump in to defend your character instead of hearing what they have to say.

Melissa:

For a long time, I feared being called a nag. Even though Kevin never outright called me a nag when I asked him to do something, he liked to say, "I'll do it so I don't have to hear your mouth." I didn't want to hear him say that sentence or anything like it, so I learned not to speak up when something bothered me. The problem is, after enough time passes, the floodgates open and it all pours out.

Another potential danger of name-calling is that the insult not only hurts your spouse but also often catches them completely off guard. Your partner might not have known that you thought they were a terrible cook or boring at parties. But as soon as you say it, you've made the argument larger and harder to recover from. For instance, if you're arguing about whose turn it is to pick up the kids from soccer practice and your spouse says, "Fine, I'll go since you're a terrible driver anyway," the smallish argument will likely blossom into a real fight. Sometimes we say things in jest that we really feel. And we don't want to admit it, but we sneak barbs in like we're kidding when it's clear that we most certainly are not. Any which way, avoid the name-calling, no matter the tone.

Kevin:

Though we've never called each other names, other parts of fighting fair have come harder for Melissa and me. We were guilty of starting sentences with "You always" or "You never." We did a lot of blaming and used blanket and accusatory statements, which made the accused partner go on the defensive.

Nowadays, we work to say, "I feel like this" or "When you say that, it makes me feel like this" or even something as therapized as "The narrative I'm telling myself is this." By using this phrasing, you allow your partner to understand what you're feeling and then act accordingly. The way you feel is always valid but not always warranted. So, if I say to Melissa, "The narrative I'm telling myself is that you'd rather hang out with Danni than be with me," she can either tell me why my take on things is not accurate or make an adjustment based on the way I'm feeling.

Obviously, this kind of language didn't come naturally to us. Melissa listened to podcasts about relationships and learned effective language and tactics. I was not out searching for this kind of information, but she shared her education with me, and I know good advice when I hear it. Melissa led the charge on our getting better at fighting, and I was glad to jump in and make the effort. But this all came later in our relationship. Early on, we just vented to our friends about each other.

3. Manage the Temperature of the Argument

Arguments often escalate because of built-up emotions, and you end up saying things that you can't take back. An argument about taking out the garbage might escalate to how he never helps at home, is a terrible husband, and undoubtedly learned it all from his dad, who is a selfish, egomaniacal chauvinist pig. Explosions like this result from pressure building up without an outlet.

We recommend managing the temperature with weekly or monthly check-ins. And you don't have to focus on the stuff that isn't clicking. In fact, it's better if you don't use the check-ins as an opportunity to voice all your gripes. In addition to discussing the issues that concern you, tell your partner what they do that is making you happy and what you appreciate. It can go something like this: "You really are such a thoughtful person, and I appreciate that you always ask me about my day. That's why it disappoints me when you don't remember our anniversary."

Kevin:

I once heard advice that I thought was the key to fighting fair. If you are arguing with someone, ask them this question: "Are you going to allow me a chance to explain my perspective and my side of the story, or would you just rather say what you have to say?" I think it's valuable, because oftentimes people are going off on you and they don't even realize they're not taking the time to hear your point of view. If you shine a light on the fact that a disagreement involves two sides of the story and that both voices need to be heard, you'll have a better chance of hearing and being heard. If you say that sentence out loud, your partner will more likely take a pause and listen.

Melissa:

I once saw a meme that speaks to this rule of fighting fair: "Explain your anger instead of expressing it, and you will find solutions instead of arguments." Often when we fight, the anger is there, but the language to explain it isn't—and that's a key reason why an argument can escalate. It's okay to be mad, but don't take it out on your partner. Emotions and feelings are real, and you are entitled to them, but that doesn't mean you should let those things take control over you.

4. You're Never Right at the Top of Your Lungs

When you yell at someone, it puts them on defense mode. Even if your point is right, the other person will perceive you as wrong if you lose control of your tone. The words you say will have little impact if the recipient is focused on the unnecessary volume.

Melissa:

I have a thing about organizing Tupperware and cabinets. I am wholly satisfied when everything is put away in its proper place and even more satisfied when I succeed in creating that Pinterest-y vibe. Likewise, I admit I can sometimes let anger consume me when my Tupperware pieces are all over the place.

Most kitchens have a drawer or shelf or cabinet where all the plastic containers and lids are kept. Every time I open that messy cabinet in my kitchen, I say to myself, *I'm going to get to work organizing those pieces.* One time, I actually stopped and did it. I spent the time throwing away the ones that had spaghetti sauce stains and the ones that had been melted by the stove. I kept the pretty ones and matched all the lids. By the time I was finished, it looked like Marie Kondo herself had paid me a visit.

Not only did no one in my household appreciate it; they didn't maintain my system. Ten minutes after Kev, Isaiah, and Joe had entered the kitchen, the lids were separated from the bottoms and the pieces were scattered about. I started yelling at everyone about Tupperware tops. They all looked at me with blank stares, like the emoji with no mouth.

My anger was really about feeling unappreciated and the lack of care I felt from my husband and sons about something that was important to me. I wanted them to appreciate that I took the time to make our kitchen look nice. I wanted them to show that appreciation by keeping it nice. None of that came through, of course, because all they heard was this crazy lady yelling at the top of her lungs about Tupperware.

5. Stop Being Mad While You're Still Mad

It takes a lot to be the bigger person and serve up a peace offering. And we think it's one of the central tenets of fighting fair. After all, being mad is exhausting. Everyone is better off once it's over. If your partner is the one who offers a peace treaty, accept their offering. We suggest being the first one to move toward reconciliation.

Kevin:

You really have to decide not to be mad, even if you're well within your rights to still be angry. My go-to tactic to stop being mad happens in bed. If we go to bed beefing, I will turn to Melissa and say, "You know we should really have sex just to make sure we're still a unit and we're still cool." That will often get a chuckle out of Melissa, even if we don't end up having the suggested sex. (Although I'm usually very serious about having the sex, just so you know.) Or, if it's not a bedtime problem, I'll say, "You hungry? I'm going to get some wings, and you're not going to eat any of my wings if you don't talk to me." It's a tension breaker, a reminder that we're on the same team. But it doesn't mean we simply move past the thing we were fighting about. I still want to have the necessary conversation, but I start with a food offer. Saying it out loud usually eases my own tension too.

Even when Melissa and I are beefin', even when I'm resenting her, I still don't want to throw her to the wolves. One day, Melissa was making me mad, but it was an important photo shoot day for her. I was out getting food, and I happened to be driving her car. I thought, *This doggone girl has got on my nerves, but let me make sure she has an oil change and a full tank of gas. I don't want her to run out of gas or mess up her engine. Ugh . . . she got on my nerves, but I want her to be safe.* Even when we're upset at each other, I don't wish the worst for her. Melissa has done that for me countless times. And you know what happens? You get so busy taking care of each other that you stop being mad.

6. Don't Get Physical

Getting physical is unacceptable. Period. End of story. And we're not even talking about physical violence. That's an obvious nonstarter. When we talk here about getting physical, we're referring to punching a wall, throwing objects, that kind of thing. If you resort to expressing yourself physically, it's a version of a temper tantrum. Getting physical is a sign that you need to develop your verbal communication skills.

We often use the Junto Emotion Wheel[1] to put names to our emotions. The wheel works from the inside out, starting with the basic, broad spectrums of feelings and providing more specific terms for feelings within each spectrum. For example, instead of telling your partner you're sad, you might say you're regretful; instead of explaining that you're scared, you may tell your spouse you feel helpless. It's useful in assigning descriptive words to your emotions. And before you throw your iPhone across the room, go back and read the chapter about effective communication. Maybe twice.

7. Don't Shut Down

Melissa:

I shut down a lot. I'm not proud of it, but it's my automatic reaction when I'm feeling overlooked. I've realized that shutting down is often simply part of my process. When I'm angry and emotional, I get flooded and I don't want all of that to come out. I need to organize my thoughts, and I can't discuss or even argue until I've gone through my process. I'm a crier as well, so

I don't want to talk when I'm all in it—I'm sobbing, I'm not making sense, and I've got a headache. It's just a lot. I used to try to talk to Kevin while I was crying and emotional, and we never got anywhere. I just blubbered nonsensically.

When I shut down, I'm not looking for Kev to come make nice or soothe me. I need to detox, calm down, and let my emotions settle. I need to take the time to think about why I'm mad so I can come back and have an articulate, effective conversation. If Kev comes knocking on my door before I'm ready, it will make me shut down even more.

Here's an example of something that could make me shut down. As a rule, Kev is the fun parent and good cop, which means I'm often left playing the role of enforcer. I'm the one making the kids do their homework and their chores, and Kev gets to cruise in with a brand-new PlayStation. When moments arise where we are not a united front as parents, where Kev is playing video games with the boys and I have to yell at them to study for a test, I get angry and flooded with emotions. I feel sad, I feel unsupported, I feel embarrassed . . . The list goes on. If it's an isolated incident, after I've processed everything and calmed down, I want to just move past it and not bring it all up again. However, if it's an ongoing issue, something that has happened too many times, I'll go back to Kevin to discuss it rationally.

One ongoing issue is that I often feel that Kev discounts my suggestions and advice about work and then turns around and accepts the same suggestion from someone else. A few years ago, we were working on a show where little kids would be mentored by comedians. I suggested privately to Kevin that we structure the show kind of like *American Idol*. When I tell you I was argued down! Kevin said flat out that it wouldn't work because the kids would have to spend too much time in the studio. At the next meeting with our business partners, one of them made the exact same suggestion about structuring the show like *American Idol*. Kevin said it was a brilliant idea, and he embraced it wholeheartedly.

That was a huge trigger for me. And I had to address it head-on. Shutting down was not an option. In specific and concrete terms, I pointed out what had just happened and how it made me feel, and we had a detailed, healthy conversation about it. I said, "I need you to understand that two weeks ago, I suggested almost verbatim what was suggested today and you weren't with it. Now that someone else is pitching it, you're totally on board. Do you understand that my feelings are based on real actions?" He got it. Once you recognize your triggers, you must do something about them. I am currently working on speaking up once I've had time to process and think through my feelings.

Here's another story: When we were under quarantine, Kevin and I found our dream house. We loved it, it was in our price range, it looked like everything was moving forward, and then it all fell through. Because of the financial fallout of the pandemic, mortgage companies were reluctant to give loans to people who were self-employed. After we got the news that we were losing the house, Kev was able to bounce back and move on. He just figured we'd get another house soon enough. I was heartbroken, but I didn't feel safe enough to have that conversation with Kevin. Without telling Kev, I went over to the house by myself to say goodbye to it. I was angry, but I didn't allow myself to have that conversation with Kevin because I was afraid it would turn into a fight. If I could go back in time, I would say, "I feel dismissed that I have sad feelings about this house." I was sad about two things: losing the house and the fact that I couldn't share my feelings and my process with Kev.

I need to work on identifying and articulating my feelings so that I'm not dealing with them alone.

Relationship Check-In

- Do you have unresolved feelings about something that your spouse said or did that was never addressed?
- Are you creating a safe space to share your thoughts and feelings?
- Are you afraid to argue?
- When was the last time you and your partner argued silently about something?

Chapter Eight

Parenting Be Hard

Because we grew up ignorant about sex, we wanted to make sure our sons had more information, education, and freedom to express their curiosities than we did at their age. As kids grow up, the conversations about most things evolve and deepen, but this is especially true when talking to your children about their bodies. Now that we have two teenagers, we have seen that those conversations are fluid. The way we approach and respond to our kids around the subject of sex keeps changing, and we're along for the ride, making sure they know we will continue to be open, honest, and nonjudgmental about the subject. That doesn't mean it's easy, particularly since we had no role models to emulate.

On our podcast, we talked to Melissa Pintor Carnagey, a licensed social worker and the creator of Sex Positive Families, a source of education that helps parents raise children who are sexually healthy. She believes that all children deserve holistic, comprehensive, and shame-free sex education, and when we talked with her, she emphasized that it's important for our children to know their bodies, to know pleasure, and to not rely on someone else to tell them what feels good. She wisely pointed out, "If they know what feels good, they also know what does not feel good. That's how kids stay safe." We want our kids to be safe. We also want them to be informed, smart, and respectful—and ultimately, to grow up to have healthy sex lives. That's a tall order.

Kevin:

I always knew I was a pretty sexual guy. I mean, in kindergarten, I was kissing girls under the blanket during nap time. But when I was growing up, there was no conversation about sexual health and safety. It was just, "Don't have sex because you're going to get somebody pregnant, and I ain't gonna help you take care of that baby." I learned zero from my parents. By middle school, I had learned about sex for real—but even then, all the information came from my friends, movies, television, and magazines. One time, my homeboy got his hands on a porn tape, and like so many seventh-grade boys do, we all sat up in a room watching that porn movie and proceeded to dream great dreams.

In eighth grade, we took a sex ed class, but masturbation was not covered in the curriculum and my parents certainly never talked about it. My best friend became the de facto expert on this and all other taboo subjects.

"Have you ever jacked off?" he asked one day when we were at my house.

"Nah," I said.

"When you get hard, you gotta rub your meat until you ejaculate."

Well, I knew about wet dreams from sex ed, and by golly, I loved how wet dreams felt. *You mean to tell me I can do that anytime? Point me in the right direction of that.*

"You need some liquid."

"Why?"

"You can't just do it dry; it won't feel good."

"What do I use?"

"Dishwashing liquid."

Dishwashing liquid. I kid you not. I didn't even bat an eye. To be fair, I was poor and Black. We used dishwashing liquid for everything: washing dishes, drawing bubble baths, making the bubbles for a car wash, cleaning our hands at the kitchen sink (which I still do to this day). Literally everything. *Nice,* I thought, *another great way to use Ajax. What a versatile and handy household product!* Immediately after my buddy told me about this wonderful new way to make the most of the dish soap, I came up with an excuse to kick him out of my house so I could do a little experimenting at 3:28 in the afternoon.

I grabbed the dish soap from under the kitchen sink and went straight into my bedroom, where I worked to conjure up some images in my mind. I got hard and immediately started rubbing blue Ajax all over my meat. *Aggressively.* I figured it had to be rough like all the sex portrayed in the porn I had seen. I was wrong. It did not feel good at all. I tried it a little softer, but by then the Ajax started to burn my little weenie. So I gave up on this experience and took a cold shower, both to calm my loins and also to cool my peen from the unfortunate reaction. My walk of shame was returning that blue soap to the kitchen and putting it back under the sink. I walked around the rest of the week with a peen as red as a hot dog.

That, ladies and gentlemen, is a true story and the reason you should talk to your kids about sex. If you don't give them accurate information, they will get it from some stupid kid. If you don't provide a safe place to verify or debunk foolish ideas, then it's your own fault if the dish soap goes missing.

Melissa:

Sex ed was offered in middle school as part of our PE class. I have no idea why those two were linked, but I guess they were both about our bodies, so the topics got smashed together. To participate, we had to bring a permission slip home for our parents to sign. My godbrother's parents refused to sign it, and I was convinced my mom and dad were going to do the same. I was anxious. I knew very well that I was naïve and needed to be educated. At that point, I had had no conversations about sex, even with friends, even on sleepovers. And though I never would've admitted this, deep down inside I was curious. Shockingly, my parents signed, giving their permission.

That class was yet another abstinence-driven lesson about sex. I remember them showing us an anatomical sketch of a penis. I was like, *Oh my God, they're actually showing us this!* I wondered if it was porn. Other than that, though, there really was no useful information about alternatives to abstinence. It didn't satisfy my buried, unspoken curiosity.

When the movie *Soul Food* came out in 1997, I was in ninth grade. My sister and I watched the movie at my pastor's house with his children. When the sex scene was about to start, the other kids were on high alert: "It's about to happen; it's about to happen." I excused myself from the room. I knew I could not, would not, watch it—because if I actually saw a sex scene, I would be tainted.

It wasn't until tenth grade that the subject of sex came up again. Our church's first lady gave talks from the pulpit or in teen Bible study, and she once said, "If any of y'all are having sex, I pray that God reveals it." Essentially, she said that if we were having sex, she prayed for us to get pregnant. The irony was that her teenage son got a girl pregnant sometime later. Her prayer fell on her house, but it also fell on mine because my little sister found out she was pregnant on the day of her high school graduation (goodbye, college track scholarship). The first lady's talk terrified me and made me put up barriers to sex, even though I was nowhere near having it myself. The scare tactic was enough!

Kevin:

I was a latchkey kid, so my brother and I had a little too much freedom when we weren't at school. We had dirty magazines. We flipped through Cinemax and the other high-number channels that didn't come in clearly, looking through waves of static for a boob.

As an adult, I wanted the subject of sex and sexuality to be handled differently for our boys than it was for me when I was growing up. It's not like our pastors and parents set out to teach us wrong on purpose. I don't think anyone does that. I'm sure the grown-ups in my life had the best intentions, but like a lot of people, they made mistakes. And our pastor had the power to truly shape our views about sex and our bodies because we put so much faith in him. We regarded him as a therapist, a financial adviser, and a sex-ed teacher. Our pastor taught us what he understood to be true. His message was clear: abstinence only. That's how it was. But it's not what I wanted for my kids.

The problem is, no one in our lives modeled open and honest parenting for us. I was trained more thoroughly to put burger patties on a grill at Burger King than I was to raise human beings. I wanted to talk to my kids openly so they knew they could come back to me with the same amount of openness about what was on their minds. As Melissa Pintor Carnagey says, sex talks are "only awkward if we keep them awkward."[1]

I want my boys to get married first, then have sex, then have kids. But I also want them to be free of the ignorance, fear, and shame that surrounded my early sexual life. I had a lot of shame when it came to sex, yet I still did it. Melissa and I try to impart our values with a holistic approach to sexuality. We educate our sons, make our values clear to them, and then set them free in the world to make their own choices. It's kind of like the approach Italian people use when it comes to wine. Italian parents typically don't make drinking wine something their kids have to abstain from. It's part of the culture, and as a result, there is less curiosity, less alcoholism, and fewer alcohol-related deaths than in America.[2]

When the boys were ten and twelve, we sat down with them to talk about sex—before they even asked. It might have been a little early, but we wanted to get ahead of it and prevent the ignorance we experienced. Melissa and I told our sons about protection. We discussed the dangers of mixing sex with alcohol and drugs, how substances pretty much erase any chance of consent. We told them the dangers of a one-night stand. I said to them, "You have a better chance of a successful sexual experience if you are in a committed relationship. If you're not in an exclusive relationship with someone you know well and who knows you well, your chance of having her feel differently about whatever goes on between you is much higher. If she feels differently than you do, you are potentially going to be in a lot of trouble. Here's how you mitigate risk: no alcohol, no drugs, no sex with a person you just met." We even checked in with them about homosexuality. All the above is on the opposite end of the spectrum from anything we grew up talking about with our parents.

I want our boys to own their sexuality. I want them to be proud of it, but I also want them to honor sex as something God designed to take place in marriage. While I do want them to wait, I also recognize that their reverence for sex may look different from mine, so if they decide to have sex in a committed relationship outside marriage, that will have to be. I just hope that sex for them will serve as a way to connect emotionally, a way for them to build a real relationship with someone.

Melissa:

From the time I was a young girl until my wedding day, I tried to tamp down my curiosity around sex, but I was just hiding the fact that I was interested in learning about it. As Melissa Pintor Carnagey says, "Not talking about sex creates an untapped curiosity." I'm here to tell you, firsthand, there are no truer words!

On *The Love Hour,* Ms. Carnagey explained that our bodies are not shameful; they're natural, and they have functions. It is up to us, as parents, to instill this information in our kids so that we don't rely on the world to teach them. Of course, our kids will hear chatter from untrusted sources (like other kids on the playground), and the hope is that they know they can bring it back to us so we can inject our own values into the conversation. For instance, if our son tells us he heard that sex is when "a boy puts his penis in a girl's vagina," we can provide an improved version that includes our values: "Sex is when a husband and wife love each other very much and want to be close. And then, yes, the husband puts his penis in his wife's vagina as part of sexual intercourse."

See the difference? If our kids can really trust that we're straight with them, we will have greater influence than all the playground talk they hear. I want to have the opportunity to respond to their curiosities so I can circle our moral values but without guilt, negativity, or shame.

We learned from Carnagey that if we start these conversations with our children early, we build a healthy foundation for openness and accuracy. These discussions are layered. The early conversations aren't about sex as much as they're about creating body awareness. We use the correct terminology about body parts and functions, and we answer their questions honestly. It's our job to prepare kids for a healthy sense of their bodies and sex, more than it is our job to ensure they remain virgins until their wedding days.

My main message when discussing sex with my boys has been about giving them agency, voicing normalcy, and emphasizing consent. In fact, the first time the subject of consent came up was kind of by accident. Isaiah was thirteen, and one of his close friends, who happens to be a girl, wanted to sleep over at our house along with a few of his other friends, who are boys. I immediately sat Isaiah down and explained why this was a hard and fast *no* from me. I said that if she spent the night, she (and to some extent, Isaiah) would be putting herself in a precarious position. We've all read the stories in the news about situations where a girl or woman is alone with a group of guys and things get out of hand. Even though I knew in my heart that nothing bad would happen with Isaiah and his friends that night, I figured it's never too soon to teach him to ask himself if he's putting himself and others in the best situation. He was confused and a little bummed, because he was young and he just wanted all his friends to be together. But he understood. It was our first conversation about consent, and it came up authentically and organically.

Even as a grown, married woman, I feel like I am still establishing my own agency over my body and the fact that I deserve to feel pleasure. I want to ensure that my boys understand those things at a young age. I try to communicate that sex and sexual feelings are normal. As Michelle Hope says, "We are sexual be-ings from womb to tomb." I don't want my kids growing up feeling like it is wrong or sinful when their bodies operate just as God intended.

Kevin:

Speaking of embracing how our bodies were designed to oper-ate, I'm going to return to the masturbation subject, this time with respect to how we've discussed it with our children. I know I may get some hate for this, but we are only honest and vulner-able in this book, so I need to keep it real here too. Growing up, I was taught that masturbation was a sin. In fact, as a teenager, I felt guiltier for masturbating than I did for having premarital sex. I knew people were having sex, but masturbation? Are you crazy? There was no way anyone else was doing this shameful thing that I was.

As we've grown as a couple, and mostly since we've done *The Love Hour,* Melissa and I have spoken to experts, including Christian sexologists, about this topic. Everything I've learned since then is that masturbation is a healthy and necessary part of a well-rounded sexuality. It is a safe way to get to know your body. However, I'm not comfortable with my boys accessing porn as part of their masturbation. I have explained that porn will give them a skewed view of sex and sexuality. I said, "I ain't trippin' if you're in the shower and you're feelin' a way, but I'm not okay with you pulling up videos on Pornhub." Also, we discussed frequency of masturbation. They should never be doing it so much that it impedes or affects any other part of their lives.

Melissa and I think differently now than we did growing up. Plus, it's hard to browbeat a kid with rules from a world they don't live in. Our kids go to church once a week. Melissa and I went at least five times every week, and we also spent time in youth groups that doubled down on the abstinence conversation. I feel like the youth group's whole point was to take you to a baseball game and then tell you not to put your bat near no balls. So, I went against what I was taught and imparted to our boys what I now believe about masturbation.

It was not an easy decision. I struggled with whether to discuss masturbation with our sons and whether to write about it here. I kept thinking about the scripture that was used to teach me that masturbation was wrong. While we were sitting there talking with the boys, I kept thinking, *Spilling seed! Don't be spilling seed!* In case it's been a minute since you've read the Bible, when Onan had sex with his brother's widow, Tamar, he withdrew before he ejaculated, and God condemned him for spilling his seed on the ground.[3] I was raised to believe that masturbation was spilling seed, and therefore, it was divinely prohibited.

Now I understand that verse to mean that if a man's brother died, he was to marry the widow and not pull out. He was to ensure that he gave her children, because in that culture, children were one's main source of support in old age. Those cultural customs don't apply anymore. Neither of my kids is obligated to marry their brother's wife, and I need to let them spill seed if they so please. Responsibly, of course.

This has been a part of parenthood where I've wondered if I'm doing it exactly right. I'm not an authority; I'm just trying to be a good father and set my kids up for success. I wrestle with what I was taught as a kid, what I did as a kid that was different from what I was taught, and what I have learned as an adult. Some pastors say masturbation is normal and healthy, and yet plenty of people still say it's wrong. I hope I'm doing the best with my children, helping them forge healthy relationships with sex, with God, and with their bodies. I am not a theologian, so I don't exactly know. Hopefully God knows my heart and knows my sons' hearts, and hopefully we all get to go to heaven. Time will tell.

Melissa:

As the boys grew from little kids to adolescents, the conversation around sex changed. When they were small, it was about their bodies: what's natural and how people shouldn't be touching them in places that their bathing suits covered. We did our best to make it abundantly clear that they could come to us if anyone made them feel uncomfortable. Now, since they're teenagers, we check in with them often about sex and consent. I emphasize that their yes means yes and their no means no and that the same is true for the words they hear from their potential partners. I hope that our conversations, as well as their life experiences, will make them feel confident enough to say no but vulnerable enough to say yes.

Kevin:

It's important to stay current when talking to your kids, because they'll tune out as soon as you sound like an old person. I try to make sure the conversations get updated as the world changes—kinda like how I stay on top of my iPhone updates.

Some parents think that if they discuss sex with their children, they are tainting their kids by introducing a dangerous topic or pushing them down an immoral path. You might think, *I don't want to have the conversation because I don't want them even thinking about it.* Having these conversations is an acknowledgment that our kids are growing older and that we, their mothers and fathers, are losing control. It's a tough thing to accept, but the sooner you get beyond that fear, the sooner you can do a much-needed service for your children.

When we first sat down with Isaiah and Joey, they weren't even teenagers yet. We all gathered in Melissa's office. Melissa and I were sitting in the chairs, being all official about the whole thing. Isaiah was lying on the floor, staring at the ceiling. He did not look away from that ceiling the whole time. I think he was terrified of making eye contact with us. Joe was sitting crisscross applesauce on the floor against the wall. He managed to make more eye contact than Isaiah did, but for the most part, his eyes were glazed over. They listened intently, but they definitely did their share of cringing. I could tell they just wanted to get outta Dodge.

Now that they're older, we've had conversations with them about porn, sex, and dating. Not surprisingly, they already knew all too well about porn. They've told us their friends watch it, which means our boys have probably dabbled in those videos. I've explained that those are paid actors, that what they might see on Pornhub isn't an accurate account of sex. I wanted to make sure my kids understood that if they watch porn, they are watching professionals re-create something that is not going to be as smooth for them in their real lives. More than likely, it ain't going to last that long. They're not going to get thirty minutes to an hour out of no teen peen. I don't want them expecting their first time (or any time really) to be like that. Sex is bumpy.

When Melissa and I first kissed, our teeth clanged against each other's. It was embarrassing—and that was with someone I knew and felt comfortable with. Figuring out how to do the sex stuff can be awkward. Your body will betray you. I wanted my boys to know that they will not be smooth operators the first time out of the gate. If they're with someone safe and forgiving, it will lessen any humiliation.

The sad truth is that having conversations about undoing the potential damage of porn is a necessary part of talking to your kids about sex. It's not ideal. None of this is. But when you sign up for this parenting thing, you are enrolling for the good, the bad, and the ugly. Even the conversations about bumping uglies.

Relationship Check-In

- Do you remember how you learned about sex?
- How do you want your kids to learn about sex?
- What are the most important things you want your kids to know about sex?

Chapter Nine

Quarantine Be Hard

Before you get married, you and your partner are likely to envision, and hopefully discuss, a whole range of scenarios that you'll face in your life together: starting a family, building your careers—you get the idea. You might ask each other a bunch of what-ifs, testing the waters to see if you have similar points of view. Then, you get married and you brace yourself for sudden shocks like unexpected pregnancy, financial changes, or illness that put your bond to the test. But until March 2020, you probably didn't think to consider what a year of quarantine might do to your relationship. We certainly didn't. It was all new territory, and we had no established framework with which to approach it.

The world changed for everyone, and marriages were put to the test. Suddenly, people who were accustomed to spending their days apart and reuniting at the dinner table were in each other's faces 24/7. It was a whole lot of togetherness, and that's not always a good thing. For us, Covid-19 presented challenges we could never have predicted. The pandemic became the manifestation of the inner war that was happening between us. All the conversations and lessons we've shared in this book, from communication to fighting to sex, were brought up for us once again—and compressed into a year of quarantine. It turned out to be the very thing we needed. The shutdown was a springboard from which we homed in on the problems in our relationship and set on a path to fixing them.

Melissa:

Quarantine affected our marriage the way heat affects glass. When glassblowing, you must apply heat for the glass to be manipulated. When the heat is turned up, the raw material of the glass becomes malleable. Then, once things are in position, exactly the way you want them, you remove the glass from the heat, and it hardens and stabilizes.[1] Quarantine was like that. It changed things that were previously in place, or so we thought. But it also forced issues that were below the surface to come up and be dealt with.

Kevin and I experienced the effects of the pandemic very differently. I had big feelings about all of it, and to be fair, I didn't do a good job of communicating my feelings to Kev.

By February 2020, I was finding my groove as an entrepreneur. The *Love Hour* podcast was two years old, and I had what I thought was a brilliant idea: combining a live Love Hour event with a wedding vow renewal.

I have a few regrets about my wedding day. The first is that my dad was on active duty and couldn't be there to walk me down the aisle. The second, and far less noble, regret was that I hated the way I looked on my wedding day. My hair, my dress, and my makeup were all lacking. My dress was never properly altered to fit my small frame, and the extra material just kind of hung on me in a way that did nothing for my figure. The hairdresser was late and pressed for time; she ended up sticking this weave in my head that wasn't even curled or styled. I had rocked short hair for quite some time and was not a long-hair person, so I didn't even know what to do with it. It made no sense.

I had been dying for an opportunity to do all those things right, and I figured probably many other brides and grooms felt the same. So I planned a three-day event in Atlanta, Georgia, that would include a vow renewal ceremony for 250 couples, officiated by Kevin. The rest of the conference would be educational but also supplemented with comedy shows, date-night activities, and a big 1990s-themed party.

Being busy gives me meaning. I find value in doing and creating, and I was absorbed in all the planning for the conference. I had the décor picked out and everything. It felt meaningful to have a creative work outlet that was all mine—something that didn't involve Kevin. Then quarantine hit, and my Love Hour conference had to pivot to virtual. I lost tons of money, and I was angry. That conference had given me purpose. And then it was gone.

Then there were the changes at home. Before the shutdown, we lived a very predictable, very routine life. Our days and weeks and months moved along with jam-packed calendars, and we operated as though everything between us was fine because we were too scheduled to notice any problems. And it worked. Our married life looked like a well-oiled machine. When Kevin was on the road and I was home, we each had our private time. Kevin might have used his in the hotel watching *The Office*, and I had the time to myself to get my hair and nails done. If we weren't communicating well, the distance allowed us to forget and move on. And if we got into a tiff when we were on the road together, we had to take the stage and perform, which prevented us from spending time arguing.

Before Covid-19, Kev and I were trying to get better at working as a team. We were failing miserably, but the energy and effort were there, and to some extent, that's what mattered most. Once the pandemic hit, the difficulty went up. We had to work to make our lives run with overlap instead of just running parallel to each other.

The biggest change was being home together. In the first weeks of lockdown, I felt like we should be doing fun activities as a family, since we'd never had all this time at home. I thought, *Oh, we are gonna really connect*. Instead, a couple weeks went by and that connection was not happening. Most days, I found myself alone in one part of the house while the boys were in their separate rooms with their doors closed and Kevin watched *The Office*. We were four people in four different rooms, sharing a word or two in passing with one another, but otherwise going our own ways.

One night the four of us gathered to watch *The Mandalorian*. In the episode where Luke Skywalker showed up, Kevin and the boys jumped around and high-fived each other. I couldn't participate. I just stood up and left the room, because I was too in my head about feeling lonely. I didn't know what to do about it. I didn't know how to ask for help, because I felt like I should know better. I was failing.

I have come to regard quarantine as a time when our lives were disrupted for the good. Kevin and I were on a path that was destructive, and we didn't even realize it. And when I say *destructive,* I mean it to the fullest extent of the word. Our paths in life were separating. We may not have been headed toward divorce, but we were definitely headed toward a sad, unhealthy marriage. For your marriage to not only survive but thrive, you need connection and communication, which require crisscross, overlap, and shared experiences.

Kevin:

Quarantine was for us what it was for most couples: the first time we spent twenty-four hours a day together. Prior to touring, Melissa and I both worked nine-to-five jobs. When I started touring, Melissa was still at a regular job, so even when I was in town, we saw each other only at night and one day each weekend. The time apart provided good opportunities to miss each other. After three days and no *secks*, I missed Melissa in *lust*. Coming home, I went right into the throes of passion. I had more energy to give to Melissa, and vice versa. Even little things like having some alone time in the car during my son's soccer practice allowed me to think about stuff. But in quarantine, I felt guilty indulging in personal time when it seemed like we were supposed to spend all our time together.

I realized that we didn't know how to have separate space in the same house. Before Covid, when we were both home, we happily spent that time together, hanging out. But forced to stay home together, we got on each other's nerves. I wondered if we'd been a better couple when I was home only three days a week. It's terrible to find yourself saying, "I love my wife but not seven days a week."

Melissa:

It's often said that when one part of your life is going well, the other parts suffer. So, when your career is popping, your personal life might be in shambles. When quarantine hit, I felt like all parts of my life were messy.

It wasn't until I sat down to write this chapter that I had a revelation about what I went through. It seems I definitely experienced a bit of a depression. Quarantine illuminated all my fears of entrepreneurship at once. It was a loss of identity, a loss of direction, and total confusion about what I was going to do next. I still felt relatively new to the entrepreneurial world, and it seemed like before my foothold was 100 percent secure, it was being stripped away from me. We weren't on tour, there were no plans to be on tour, and the one thing I had worked hard on for the last year—the Love Hour conference—was canceled. I had no idea what would come next. Safe to say, Covid played on my insecurities and fears. I felt like there was nothing Kev could do to make me happy. I remember crying in the shower during those first weeks of lockdown.

The sadness deepened when we lost our dream house—the one we wrote about in chapter 7, "Fighting Be Hard." For me, that house was a symbol that we had made it in Los Angeles. It was my big-girl house, and I was so excited to get it all set up and beautiful. Losing the house, in combination with losing my confidence as an entrepreneur, did a number on my self-worth. My sadness was about so much more than losing a material thing, but I felt that I couldn't speak openly to Kevin about it because I worried that he would judge me for caring too much about a house. That feeling of not being able to get my feelings out and not being understood exacerbated my feelings of isolation and loneliness.

Kevin:

Losing that house definitely added insult to injury. Here we were, under quarantine, with tours and conferences canceled and rising tension in the home. Now the one thing we were all excited about fell apart.

I had totally wrapped my arms around this new house. In fact, I started getting smoothies at the Whole Foods in the new neighborhood. For the first time in my life, I was actually going to live near a Whole Foods! Not a Vons, but a bougie Whole Foods with a deli and alkaline water and vegan doughnuts. We didn't even live there yet, and I went way out of my way, passing two Ralphs, three Trader Joe's, and four Smart & Final grocery stores to get to that Whole Foods. Even though their smoothies are terrible, I was buying them smoothies to prove a point. I belonged in this neighborhood. And then, all of a sudden, it didn't happen.

I was sad, but Melissa had put much more into the new house than I had. The house we were living in was filled to the brim with the furniture and decorations she'd already purchased for the new place. Now we had all this great stuff and no place to put it. Walking past the boxes every day was a constant reminder of the disappointment. On top of that, we had already given up the current place, so we had to leave.

Again, I was sad. But my self-image as husband, protector, and provider kicked in. I took it upon myself to find us a new place to live, but all the options were either terrible or wildly expensive. That home search brought up issues, because now our money story came into play. I wanted a house that was more expensive, and Melissa didn't think it was a good idea. I took that to mean maybe she was losing faith in me as a provider. She took it to mean I wasn't recognizing her fears.

Then, as if all that wasn't enough, I made a blunder on the *Love Hour* podcast. We were talking about marriage and sex during Covid. I had assumed that because most couples were trapped at home all the time, they were probably having more sex under quarantine than they were before. But then I read an article that said the exact opposite was true. On the podcast, I said, "Yeah, man, we're having less sex too." Melissa shot me a look that told me right away that I was in trouble. She was pissed that I was just telling our business without clearing it with her first. I have since learned that talking about your relationship in real time means that you're often discussing stuff that's still fresh, stuff that's not ready for public airing, so I need to make sure Melissa and I are both on the same page. I have made the mistake of being loyal to the joke, meaning erring on the side of having good content at Melissa's expense.

These things putting stress on our relationship—the loss of work, the home loan falling through, the misstep on the podcast—were happening *because* of Covid. It shook me. *When will things go back to normal? When will I get back to earning the money that supports my family? What if my fans forget about me? What if I never go on tour again? How will I recover from this shutdown?* I guess you can call it anxiety, and it definitely came out when Melissa and I fought. Normally, when we were beefin', we'd be on bad terms for a few hours, maybe a day. Now it was the opposite: a few good moments dropped in long spells of bad energy and silent treatment.

One day, Melissa walked by me and said, "What's wrong with me? Am I going crazy?" She hugged me and started crying. I thought about saying, "Yes, you are going crazy," but decided against it. Instead, I hugged her and let her cry. I hadn't seen her break down like that since her parents were getting divorced. (More on that in the next chapter.) In that moment I just wanted to be a support system for her.

Even though I worked hard to be present for my family, I'm not gonna lie, I missed the parts of my life that gave me time away from home. Toward the end of quarantine, a friend of mine was going on tour for the first time since be shutdown. I asked him if he was going to miss his kids and family, and his response was a resounding *no*. "I am looking forward to being away from them," he said. I was shocked. I mean, you can't say that. Not out loud.

I realized I'd been feeling that way too. Around the same

time, Melissa was going to Big Bear for a short work/girls' trip. It was a week when we weren't vibing at all. I mean, there were no good vibes to be found. All the vibes were *off*. I was so ready for a little break, two days where I would be eating popcorn, ordering pizza, and cranking up the AC in the house with no attitude from Liss. Then the cases spiked in California, and her trip got canceled. The city of Big Bear didn't allow Airbnb guests. I asked Melissa, "Are you sad that you're not going?" She said she wasn't. "Not even a little sad?" She still said no. I went on, "That's crazy that you're not sad." I wanted the break, and I wanted her to share my sentiments so I would feel less guilty about having them. Not only did I feel a little guilty; I felt stuck—stuck at home, stuck in a rut, stuck in my career.

Those were definitely new feelings. It was like we were all alone in the house, behind closed doors, yet it somehow felt we were on top of each other. A whole bunch of contradictions were hitting us all.

Melissa:

All these feelings impacted us in ways we've seen infidelity impact other marriages. In chapter 6, we explored how infidelity opens couples' eyes to problems they previously didn't address. The marriage might survive, but the relationship is forever changed; the couple will never go back to the way things were beforehand. That's what quarantine did for us: It forced us to look at ourselves, each other, and our marriage in a way that we never had before. It gave us the opportunity to say out loud, "There's a problem here." Similarly, quarantine propelled us into therapy. The lockdown brought up issues that we knew we needed a licensed professional to help us work through. Being locked down didn't solve our problems, but it was the first step in fixing them.

Two months into the shutdown, in the midst of the uneasiness and awkwardness that existed between the two of us, George Floyd was murdered. We had barely left the house since March, but protests were taking place, and it was important to us to join in. The Black Lives Matter march was our first outing since the pandemic began. We were willing to risk being exposed to the virus because it was important to us to be a part of the movement. It was a reckoning moment not only for the United States but also for me and Kev.

To be sure, George Floyd wasn't the first unarmed Black man killed at the hands of the police, but his death felt different. Growing up Black, I had heard the stories about such killings, and of course, I never doubted them. But to watch it with my own eyes, over and over again on video, was altogether different.

Our thoughts immediately went to our son Isaiah. He was doing walks around the neighborhood, and we needed to sit down and explain to him about taking his hood off his head and making sure he smiled at people. We needed to ensure that he was sharing his location with us. We even told him to call us and turn on his camera if he met someone who didn't know who he was. It was an external added layer of stress. Joey was eleven at the time, old enough to take part in these conversations. This part breaks my heart, and I'm crying as I sit here writing this. We explained the historical dynamics and told him that, as a young Black boy, he needed to be aware of his surroundings and that white people might look at him differently. He broke down crying and said, "But I just don't understand. I didn't do anything. What if I didn't do anything wrong?" That broke my heart wide open.

I felt the shift in our culture and in America, and I wanted to be a part of it and set an example to our boys. Kevin and I left the boys at home and went to the march. I thought, *This is what it must have been like to go to marches in the civil rights movement.* It felt like I was in the middle of a historical moment, that I was taking part in something important. I was pleasantly surprised to see people of all different races there. Members of the LGBTQ community were holding signs where the word *Black* was in written in rainbow colors. We ran into people we knew: one friend from college who was part of the Black Student Union with us and one of Kevin's comedian friends who was there with his wife. We all marched together.

We took part in the chants. At first, Kevin and I and the people around us didn't know the words, but suddenly, as if by some innate understanding, we knew what to say and when to clap. As soon as someone grabbed the bullhorn, everyone locked in on that person in harmony, in synergy. It was beautiful. We walked for close to four hours, wearing our masks on that hot Los Angeles day. By the time the sun was going down, we made our way home.

Kevin:

When we got back from the march, we downloaded to our kids. It wasn't the first conversation we had had with our boys about this issue, but because it was happening to kids Isaiah's age, it was yet *another* conversation we needed to have. We didn't have the luxury of waiting until they were older, until they were driving. Tamir Rice was twelve when a Cleveland police officer shot and killed him. Our son Joe was eleven. I broke down toward the end of the conversation. I tried so hard to be strong for them, but when my youngest burst into tears, I felt helpless and I just lost it. I broke down to the point that Isaiah held me in his arms while I sobbed. It was such a vulnerable moment.

In *Do the Right Thing,* Spike Lee paints a picture that I think is similar to what we all felt during the pandemic. In the movie, it's summer in New York. The temperature is in the high nineties, tensions are high, and then some teens pry open a fire hydrant. For me, George Floyd's murder felt like the moment the water started bursting out. Because it wasn't just George Floyd. It was Eric Garner, Trayvon Martin, Michael Brown, Tamir Rice, Walter Scott, Alton Sterling, Philando Castile, Sandra Bland, Breonna Taylor. It was name after name, scenario after scenario. And at home, Melissa and I were dealing with uncertainty about our careers, sadness about losing the house, and feelings we had never had about each other. It was *a lot*!

I would say my marriage advice after going through a year of quarantine is this: Expect everything to stay the same while being prepared for everything to change. Your marriage will be tested on how you navigate things you never planned on navigating. And we've gone through plenty of challenges that were just as tough as a year of a pandemic. You never know what's around the corner, but you know you're going to go through it together.

Melissa:

As we write this, the restrictions due to Covid-19 have lifted considerably, but the world is still dealing with the virus. Along the same lines, Kevin and I started addressing our problems in quarantine, but they are by no means fixed. We still have bad days, we still fall into the same traps, and we still display some of the same bad behaviors. But we are more aware now than we used to be. Those behaviors surface less frequently, they don't last as long, and they are less intense. Our work in therapy is still very much in process. We're better today than we were in March 2020, but we've got more work to do.

To Kevin's points above, I would add that we all need to

make sure we're working out the stuff below the surface. Sometimes all the errands and plans and other things you do to keep busy cover up the resentment, the unresolved issues, and the unmet needs. Don't wait until a global pandemic forces you to deal with that stuff. Tune in to your feelings, your stresses, how life changes are affecting you. Articulate those feelings to your partner before they blow up. Don't stay silent, even if you think doing so protects your partner and your marriage. We made the mistake of using that excuse to explain our silence, and it made our issues more pronounced. Surprises in a marriage can be exciting and beneficial (a surprise gift, a surprise love note, a surprise sexual advance), but a surprise about uncomfortable or unhappy feelings does your marriage no favors.

Relationship Check-In

- How did the pandemic affect your marriage?
- What did quarantine teach you about yourself and your spouse?
- If you were to go back into quarantine, what would you do differently before, during, and after?

Chapter Ten

Divorce Be Hard

A constant thread in scripture is that marriage is a lifelong commitment. The belief is that God unites and blesses the newly married couple in a spiritual way, and that blessing comes with a deep sense of responsibility. We are instructed to love our spouses just as Christ loved the church, which means giving up everything for our partners. It says in the Bible, "They are no longer two, but one flesh."[1] In other words, your commitment to your spouse should be just as permanent as your ties to your mama and your granddaddy. And of course, his blessing allows the couple to celebrate that unity with sexual intercourse. Thank you, God!

When we were growing up, a popular saying was "Divorce is not an option." We heard those words over and over again, at church and at home, and we also remember adults joking about death being the only way out of their marriages. But the sad truth is, sometimes, despite your best efforts, divorce is the only way out of a marriage that is unfixable.

In this chapter, we'll debunk the cliché about divorce not being an option while providing advice and tips to protect your marriage from divorce. Despite the fact that divorce happens to be a very real option, we want you to leave no stone unturned keeping your marriage intact. And we've come to believe that there's power in facing that hard truth head-on.

Melissa:

When you grow up in the church and have parents who are saved, you might assume, even into adulthood, that marriage is impenetrable. After all, the Bible says, "What God has joined together, let no one separate."[2] Getting divorced means taking a sacred knot, a knot tied in front of God and family and friends, and pulling on all the threads to completely unravel it. I grew up hearing over and over again, "Divorce is not an option." But then I noticed that pastors and ministers had gotten divorced. Plenty of Christians I knew had gotten divorced too. That's a fact. It happens to people.

Still, when I was growing up, and even after I embarked on my own marriage, my perspective on love and marriage was idealized. I thought those butterflies were sustainable. That sex and communication would be easy. I thought that as long as we kept God first, everything would be peaches and cream and my husband and I wouldn't go through seasons of disappointment or doubt.

Looking back, I realize not a single marriage in my family lasted "until death do us part." All my aunts, uncles, and grandparents ended up divorced. But my parents? They weren't like the others. They were Christians, and I assumed that would make all the difference. My mom got saved when I was ten, and my dad followed suit two years later, after we moved from Germany to Hawaii. I had been aware of conflicts in their marriage before then. I mean, I saw them arguing, fighting, yelling, screaming, and throwing dishes. Then suddenly, everything was perfect—at least that's how I saw it. It seemed to me that God came in and saved my parents' marriage. I honestly thought that when that plane landed in Hawaii, God entered our lives.

Well into my adulthood, divorce was antithetical to how I viewed my parents. I used to wake up with anointing oil on me—my mom would put a greasy cross on my forehead while I slept. She should have checked with a dermatologist first, because I'm sure her whole process was to blame for my acne-prone skin. She had a prayer closet with a laminated sign that said *Praying, Do Not Disturb.* She put her sign in a plastic sleeve and taped it to the door. I mean, this woman was *saved* saved. And *that* person got divorced after twenty-five years of marriage.

It was December. Kevin and I had been married two years, and I was on maternity leave after giving birth to Isaiah. One night my sister and I were at my pastor's house. Everything was decorated for the holidays, and we were all talking and having a festive time when the pastor's wife got serious and said that we needed to have a conversation. My mom arrived, they sat us down, and my mom told us that she and my father had gotten divorced in April. *Eight months earlier.* There was no room for grieving or processing. It was already done and done. That was the moment when my world got flipped upside down.

My folks' divorce rocked my entire universe. Previously, I had tried to emulate my parents' marriage, but their split brought everything into question: love, loyalty, God, and truth. And remember, my parents' marriage ended around the time Kevin was launching his comedy career. All of a sudden, I was insecure, jealous, and threatened. And while the thought of divorce had never previously entered my mind, suddenly, in the face of my parents' divorce, I began to question whether my own marriage was going to succeed.

I realized that I had been living in a fantasy bubble and that I had to adjust to a new normal, which colored my entire outlook on life. My mind was racing: If my parents were susceptible and ultimately succumbed to divorce, then so were we. If my mother and father didn't get their happily ever after, who was to say I would? Why was I exempt?

So I became suspicious. I started snooping into Kev's business like a detective, trying to gather evidence to prove he was unfaithful or dishonest or just a bad husband. I also went through a heavy season of questioning God. I remember thinking, *God, if marriage is the institution* you *created, if* you *are the one who said divorce is not an option, how are you letting this happen*? I was in a terrible slump, and I wore it every day wherever I went.

At long last, I accepted that I couldn't go back in time and change what happened to my parents. It was done, and all I could do was learn how to live with it. I adopted a new and different frame of mind. I trained myself to think like this instead: *My parents' marriage is not my marriage. I cannot let their divorce have a negative effect on my relationship. I can't wear this anymore. I can't own it. I can't let the decisions they've made become the decisions that I will make for myself. What happened to them cannot dictate and is not an indicator of what will happen to me. I have to accept that to get over what happened to them. I cannot give up on my marriage.*

Kevin:

When Melissa's parents got divorced, I was sad, but I can honestly say that I didn't think it was going to affect our marriage. When Melissa first opened up about her feelings, I remember thinking, *Girl, who are you married to? Me! You are good. You are big trippin'. This is a waste of anger.* I felt like Melissa was taking on unnecessary battles that were not hers to fight.

Of course, I also worried that as long as she stayed an emotional wreck, I wouldn't be getting the draws as a result. It was my irrational fear. I mean, I know I'm not gonna get the draws every day—and if I'm not gonna get the draws because of something I did or because she's on her period, then fine. But I'm not gonna get the draws because her parents are divorced? That might have been the thing I was most upset about. I was like, *Girl, you gotta get this together, 'cause I need what you got, and I can't get it when you're stressin'. We gotta work through this, 'cause I am hard.*

I was so naïve. It's amazing how much we frame our own life based on our parents, regardless of who we are. Your parents— single, divorced, married—are often your reference point for the world around you. But at the time, I didn't think like that. I should have been more thoughtful about the changes I began to see in Melissa: a woman who was never jealous became jealous; a woman who was so sure about us became unsure. Of course she did! The marriage that served as a model for her disintegrated right before her eyes. Naturally that would affect how she felt about her own relationship and how secure she felt with me.

Melissa:

It goes without saying that divorce is not God's ideal plan. Truth is, divorce is *nobody's* ideal plan. But in the real world, with real people, divorce is indeed an option.

Throughout my life, I have heard churchy people say that divorce is acceptable in cases of infidelity, abuse, or other serious breaches of trust that violate the marriage contract. In other words, when the marriage is already severed, divorce can be an acknowledgment that the union is broken. But it's still frowned on in scenarios where the marriage is merely disappointing or difficult. I have to ask, though, What if you are profoundly unhappy? What if you're deeply unhappy with your partner and have been for a long time, and there seems to be no end in sight for your misery?

Expectations and resentment are likely the reasons my parents' marriage failed. My mother's primary love language is quality time, but she didn't get that time from my dad. He had a more traditional male approach. He figured that if he was working and supporting the family, he was doing all that was required of him. She wanted him to call into work every once in a while and spend the day with her, but he didn't operate that way. Each resented the other for this disconnect. When my dad went overseas, my mom found someone else to give her that time. She didn't know how to express what she wanted, and he believed he was giving her everything he should simply by providing. No amount of praying or going to church could fix that disconnect.

Kevin:

I firmly believe that in some scenarios, you are better off apart than you are together. You know how when you have the flu and you're sick for a whole week, those are the longest seven days in the history of the world? For some couples, marriage is the worst flu ever, and the misery is going to last until the end of time. If you are always fighting, if you don't have common goals and life plans, if you make each other and the people around you miserable, if you've put in the work and it's not getting better, you might start viewing divorce as an option.

If you're going to bed and waking up with someone every

day, you should, for the most part, be glad that person is there next to you. I'm not talking about silly, frivolous happiness. This is not about bursting into tears of joy every morning when you smell your partner's fresh-in-the-morning scent or having butterflies every time your spouse walks into the room. That's not realistic. What's realistic is having true appreciation for each other and being glad to have each other as partners in good times and in bad.

One thing that I love about being married to Melissa is watching her sleep. She looks gorgeous when she's asleep. No drooling, no open-mouth breathing. To me, love, twenty-plus years into this relationship, is seeing her sleep peacefully and knowing that perhaps I help provide some of that peace for her. It's knowing that we work together to build a life that we are happy with, and a peaceful night's sleep is the epitome of those feelings. It's having her next to me at our son's soccer game and cheering on this little person that we made together. There's a long-term connection, a world of inside jokes between us. That's love. My heart isn't beating fast, but it's love, I'm here to tell you.

Melissa:

While we're realistic enough to admit that no one is happy with their partner all the time, we do think that in a marriage, ideally, you're happier when you're with that person than without. You may fight occasionally or have ongoing areas of disagreement, but it's not about that. It's knowing that, at the end of the day, you're glad to get home to each other.

The sad truth is that sometimes that kind of happiness disappears completely. It can be an unhappiness that grows over time and breeds anger and resentment. Other times, people stop seeing the world in the same way as their partners; they have different priorities about money, family, or work than they did when they first got married. People change, and sadly they often don't change the same way at the same time. Maybe you're not in agreement about having kids or raising kids. Maybe you realize you have conflicting views on work and finances and spending. Whatever it is, people don't just wake up one day and realize they're unhappy. It happens over years, and it gets to a point where they decide it's not working and that staying together means staying miserable.

Before I dig too deeply into the saying "Divorce is not an option," let me first say that I respect and understand the statement. I know it comes from a good place. I know the idea is to encourage a married couple to stay together no matter what. But there are two main problems with the phrase: (1) It's not true, and (2) it's actually counterproductive. When you refuse to believe divorce is an option, it suggests that your marriage will endure no matter how much or how little work you do. Resting on the idea that divorce is not an option means you can end up in a miserable marriage by believing, *You ain't going nowhere, and I ain't going nowhere.* That was the mandate we grew up with—you cannot get divorced. You would upset God, embarrass your family, and sully your name.

Against that backdrop, saying it *is* an option feels revolutionary. It honors the most important part of marriage, which is the *want*. Having that choice is what makes a marriage beautiful. Love and commitment mean I am going to honor you because I *want* to, not because I'm living by a false mandate.

When I say that divorce is an option, I am in no way advocating for it. I really believe divorce should be the very last option after you've put in the work. You need to communicate with each other about what is and isn't working for you. You must make the effort to meet your spouse's needs. You have to make your marriage a priority. You should think about seeing a therapist or a counselor or a pastor to get some third-party advice. I believe it's important to exhaust all options before you even contemplate dissolving your marriage.

A long, strong marriage can provide blessings that nothing else can compete with. Some people get divorced thinking the grass is greener on the other side of the fence and end up regretting it. Divorce also has a ripple effect. A divorce hurts a lot of people, not just the couple ending their marriage.

Marriage should not be entered into as a life sentence in which spouses are enslaved without a choice. But choosing to stay together? That's love.

Every day, Kevin and I actively and consciously choose our marriage. We choose to honor our vows and honor the rings we wear on our fingers. We intend to get all the way to "until death do us part"—and for that, we have made a choice to fight for our marriage. We've gone to therapy. We've changed the way we express our needs. We make the effort to always "choose us." When things are good, we choose our marriage. When things are bad, we choose our marriage. While Kevin would say that the most important aspect in a successful marriage is sex and I would say it's communication, the truth is that it's both— because the most important aspects of a marriage are the things that are important to the two of you.

The Greeks separated love into different categories. One was *eros*, love that is felt in the body as trembling excitement.[3] This is the love you feel when you want your spouse physically— their body, their touch—and it's strongest in the infatuation stage, early in your relationship. *Eros* love is good, but it's not enough to sustain a marriage. It fades as time passes and people get more familiar with each other. And that's okay; that's life.

Then, there's *phileo* love. Whereas *eros* love is all about the body, *phileo* love affects the soul. *Phileo* love is strong. It's the kind of love we feel when we value people as long-lasting friends.[4] Kev and I were friends before we fell in love, and we are still friends to this day. In fact, we're best friends. That friendship is always present, even when (especially when) we're not getting down and dirty.

Even though we accept that the heart-racing excitement of new love fades, we still think you should work to keep the fire alive. Don't go thinking that since the passion is going to dissipate eventually, you might as well sit on the sofa in your old sweatpants with a bowl of Pringles in your lap. That's just lazy. Don't chase the *eros* love out the door. Try your best to hold on to it. Go on a date night, get dressed up, do your hair, put on some earrings, break out a new suit and tie. Put in some effort for your lover, reminding them of all the reasons they were mad about you in the first place.

Kevin:

Let me say a little more about those butterflies I mentioned earlier. That tangible excitement of falling in love, the electricity that's depicted onscreen in every romantic comedy, is not the stuff of real, long-lasting marriage. Don't go thinking something is wrong in your marriage if you don't feel that kind of thrill as the years pass. Butterflies are mythical—at least when it comes to long-term relationships. They're about as real as hobbits and dragons, those storybook romances we saw in *The Wood* and *Sixteen Candles*. When Melissa and I were in high school and I saw her coming down the hallway, my heart started beating faster. Always. But when you spend the whole day with someone, your heart doesn't keep up that fast beat for twenty-four hours. It can't. If you got "butterflies," you probably gotta pee or fart.

We've been conditioned to expect that feeling and to think that if we don't have it, we'd better go out and try to find it. Think about how many times we've seen in movies someone waking up and kissing their partner first thing in the morning. The sun is shining, and they're in *love*. Nobody on earth would actually do that. I wouldn't kiss Melissa first thing in the morning because my breath is detrimental!

Melissa:

We can see why people get divorced. Being married for a long time is hard. Every few years, you gotta change up the way you approach your life and the life you share with your partner.

We had to make adjustments when Kev shifted from having a regular job to pursuing a career as an entertainer. I am a faithful regular at the hair salon, but I changed my routine from twice a month to once. Also, since I was the assistant manager at the bank where we had our accounts, I knew all too well that all overdraft charges were manually processed by my co-workers. I became hyperaware of our bank statement balance, checking almost obsessively, because the idea of popping up on the list of people whose accounts were overdrawn was too embarrassing to imagine. There was another season when I thought I didn't want kids, that I wanted to focus on my career. When we are married and these fundamental aspects of our beings evolve, there's always the risk that our partners might not be happy about the new versions of us. They might not want to make adjustments. They might feel like this is not the relationship they committed to, not the agreement they signed.

In every marriage, you have to learn to love your partner differently at different times. We are all constantly changing, and the fact is, personal life changes don't always include your spouse. Career and health changes happen to one person, but they will, of course, affect the entire family. The only thing you can count on is that marriage will always be work. But it's worth it.

We know that God hates divorce. The truth is, everyone hates it. We've heard Christians lament the rise of divorce, saying that too many people go into marriage thinking they have an easy way out if it doesn't work. It's like standing in line for a roller coaster knowing you can leave via the chicken exit before you actually board the ride. I think most people deserve more credit than that. It's a well-known fact that divorce is devastating. I believe most people have pure intentions, they want it to work, and they understand the gravity of marriage.

At the end of the day, we can only learn from our experiences and take the lessons with us as we move forward. These are the primary lessons I learned from my parents' divorce:

- Unspoken expectations are the quickest way to be disappointed, and disappointment often leads to resentment.
- Resentment is corrosive, meaning that, over time, it can do irreparable damage to your relationship.
- The titles *husband* and *wife* must take priority over the titles *dad* and *mom*.
- Growth, change, and evolution will happen. So choose your marriage every day. Do your best to grow and evolve together instead of separately.

For me, choosing our marriage looks like arriving home to find a white chocolate iced mocha with whip and classic oatmeal that I didn't even ask for, but Kev knows they're my favorite. It's getting extra ketchup at Chick-fil-A for Kev, even though ketchup is gross. It's showing your spouse that you are thinking of them, that you know their silly little preferences, that you have listened to their peculiar requests. It's even thanking them for walking the dog or folding the laundry, even though it's something they should be doing anyway.

We encourage all married couples to continue to choose marriage, in good times and bad. When your issues seem insurmountable, make the decision to choose each other and to work at building a better relationship that will last "until death do us part."

Relationship Check-In

- Do you view divorce as an option? Does your spouse?
- Do other people's divorces make you feel your marriage is vulnerable? Why or why not?
- What about your parents' relationship (their marriage, divorce, or lack thereof) informs your view of divorce as an option?
- Can you think of one way to choose your marriage today? How can your spouse do the same for you?

Chapter Eleven

Self-Worth Be Hard

A Love Letter from Melissa to You

There was a time, not so long ago, when the thought of loving myself was a huge mountain to climb. I grew up in a loving home, with parents who cared deeply for me and went out of their way to show it. But even if you get unconditional love from your family, society can do a real number on your self-esteem.

As a girl, I internalized a lot of society's definition of beauty and what it meant to be pretty. Beauty, in my mind, was long, silky hair, light(er) skin, and perfect teeth. When I looked in the mirror, I saw the exact opposite: an ugly duckling. There were just far too many things I believed were wrong with me. It seemed that I would be plagued by low self-esteem my entire life and that there was absolutely nothing I could do about it. I was wrong! There is absolutely something that can be done. I did it, and so can you.

On *The Love Hour,* I did a few episodes that I called "For Women Only," where I spoke directly to women, addressing common issues of insecurity and negative self-talk. Everyone has their share of insecure moments, but there's a kind of self-doubt that I think is more prevalent in women. Figuring out how to care for yourself when you're so busy caring for everyone else is a struggle. I've heard so many women express feeling guilty when they take time away from their spouse or children to do something solely for themselves. That guilt can be overwhelming.

Even though this chapter is directed at women, I think men could benefit greatly from reading the next few pages. It would be useful for the guys to understand what goes on in our hearts, our minds, and our souls. So, men: This is no time to zone out or skim or speed-read. Pay attention.

Let's start by addressing the question (you know I love to do this): *What is self-esteem?* It's the value we place on ourselves. It is made up of all our inner thoughts about who we are and what we deserve. These thoughts and feelings have a direct effect on how we behave. They come out when we're with our friends, at work, and in all aspects of our lives. And if we are lacking in self-esteem, we might not realize that we're putting ourselves down, but it emits from our every pore.

Self-esteem and self-worth, while not the same, go hand in hand. Worth is the value you place on yourself. You can feel good about yourself, but you still might accept less than you deserve because you don't adequately assess your value. Plenty of women think of themselves as smart and strong and beautiful yet still allow themselves to be treated badly. There are women who feel accomplished and capable at work, yet they still won't ask for a raise. Confidence, or lack thereof, is part of you, and you carry it no matter what you're wearing.

My lack of self-esteem began with my looks, but it extended to my personality. I wished I was funnier. I wished I was warmer.

I wished I was the person who arrived at a party and lit up the room, the person everyone wanted to be sitting next to at the dinner table. I now know to honor that Melissa is not always MrsKevOnStage, and that's okay. I also used to hate that I'm so emotional. I'm a crybaby, and I've always wished I wasn't.

For a long time, the list of things I wanted to change about myself was longer than the list of things I liked. Does that happen to you? It can take over. It can sit with you and affect how you show up in every room, no matter what kind of reaction you get from others. You might get complimented up and down, but if you don't believe it, no one else can convince you.

I hate for any woman to feel that way. That's why I launched my campaigns—mantras and commands that I've used to drum up inspiration for myself. To be clear, these campaigns are entirely personal. They were not conceived as content for social media or attempts to help anyone else find their self-love. All of this work predated social media and podcasts. I started these daily reminders long ago, when I really needed a boost, and I still use them today. They are a rallying cry for me when I am discouraged or defeated.

Quite honestly, I still struggle to feel good about myself. I still notice people who look the way I want to look, and if I'm not careful, I'll spend useless time wishing I was more like them. So I've worked to shift my standard of beauty. It took me a long time to be comfortable with my skinny body, my chocolate skin, my crooked smile, and my pudgy nose. I had a picture in my head of famous women whom I considered beautiful: Halle Berry, Tyra Banks, Cindy Crawford. None of them looked anything like me. I had to convince myself over time to accept who I am and what I look like. I realized that many women who were widely considered beautiful had chocolatey-brown skin like mine and narrow faces like mine. If I thought of them as pretty, then I should be able to think of myself that way as well.

And here's where this comes back to your marriage: I had to believe I was beautiful before I could take Kevin's word for it. Good partners will tell us we're worth it; they'll tell us they love us as we are. Those words will hit a brick wall if you don't believe it. If you're intimate with your partner and you believe you're worth it, you will show up sexy, and that is good for your marriage. If your partner tells you that you look good, you smell good, you *are* good, hopefully they're just telling you what you already know about yourself. That leads to good stuff for the two of you in every room, especially the bedroom.

The "You're Worth It" Campaign

I used to feel guilty about doing things for myself. Think about it: You're in a store and you see a cute outfit for your baby. You buy it because you know how cute the baby will look in it. But we tend not to do the same for ourselves. We go above and beyond for our kids and our husbands, but we feel guilty if we do it for ourselves.

When I was a new mom with Isaiah, I wanted him to have everything monogrammed. I wanted to see his name on *everything*. One time, I went to a trade show where they were selling VeggieTales CDs, and they offered personalized CD covers and audio files to include the child's name. The first line that played was "Hi, Isaiah! Are you ready to have some fun?" I freaked out! I had to have it! Even though it was seventy-five dollars! Now listen, in the grand scheme of things, seventy-five dollars might not be much, but for a twenty-four-year-old on a bank teller's salary, that was a lot of money for a CD. I told myself that my baby boy deserved that CD. I pulled out my debit card and took that CD home.

Conversely, around the same time, I went to the mall specifically looking to buy myself an outfit. I fell in love with a black-and-white pencil skirt in the first store I walked into. Do you ever walk around the mall not knowing exactly what you want, and when you see it, you immediately know? That was this skirt. It spoke to me. I quickly grabbed it and put it up to my waist in front of a mirror, swaying side to side, falling in love with the idea of owning it. But when I saw it was fifty dollars, I was appalled! *Who would spend fifty whole U.S. dollars on a skirt?* Surely not me! Never mind the seventy-five dollars I just spent on a CD for my one-year-old who didn't even care that they were saying his name. I immediately put the skirt down and walked to the clearance section of the store. At the time, I thought the clearance section was where I belonged. It was the only place I shopped.

To be clear, there is nothing wrong with the clearance section. I have found some fantastic things on that rack in the back of the store. But there is a difference between finding something you love that is on clearance and going to the clearance section because that is where you feel you belong.

I'm here to tell you that you are not the least important person in the house. You are not the bottom of the barrel. You are worthy of more than the clearance rack.

Later that night, I experienced the opposite of buyer's remorse: Instead of regretting a purchase I had made, I had regret for a purchase I should have made. I loved that skirt, but I let it go because I didn't think I was worth the fifty dollars. That's when I knew I had to tackle my self-esteem and self-worth from the inside out. It wasn't just about my clothes and my hair. I actually needed to deal with how I felt about, thought about, and viewed myself. I started a series of campaigns that became single points of focus for me.

Over the next year, I went through the process of finding what I call my intrinsic value: the value I have simply because I am, because I'm alive, and because I exist. It is separate from, and not dependent on, anything I've accomplished. When I regretted not buying myself the skirt, I dug deep to ask myself why I didn't think I was worth it. I questioned why I never treated myself to the best of anything. I wouldn't even order a burger with avocado because the avocado was extra. After a few months of paying acute attention to how I treated myself, it dawned on me that I had low self-esteem. It was a profound revelation! Clothes were not going to fix it. The solution had to come from the inside out.

I began affirming myself in the mirror every single day by saying out loud, "You're worth it." The mantra evolved further when Kevin and I were at a used-car lot and I saw a sign that said, *For sale. As is. No exceptions.* It struck me that whoever purchased that car would buy it, drive it, and come to love it in its current state. And I thought, *Why can't I accept myself that same way?*

When I say *as is,* I mean that you should accept yourself in whatever state of life you are in at this very moment. We tend to think that we will feel good about ourselves if we get to some not-yet-reached place in life or achieve some not-yet-attained goal. We tell ourselves, "Once I lose ten pounds . . ." or "Once I get a raise . . ." or "Once I have a baby, I'll be happy with who I am." The truth is that you are enough as you are, right here, right now. Even if nothing changes, you are worth it. You don't have to wait to feel worth it. I started by changing my mantra to *You're worth it. As is. Without change. Without exception.*

Many times, when I wasn't feeling it, I had to dig down deep to find those words. On more mornings than I can count, I looked in the mirror and forced myself to utter the words—out loud, no less—that I was worth the time it took to do my makeup and my hair and put on a nice outfit, even if I had no plans for the day. I had to say the words to myself, "Melissa, you are worth it. As is. Without change. Without exception." And I'm here to tell you that you are enough as yourself. How you feel about yourself does not improve if you slip into a designer dress or carry a Gucci purse. You have to be comfortable and confident with who you are when all the material stuff comes off.

I know this might sound like psychobabble, but after repeating this to myself daily in the mirror, I started to believe it. Take my advice. Don't just say it out loud; actually look at yourself and say it. It's powerful. I felt the shift taking place. I held my head a little higher. I walked a little taller. My confidence increased. As soon as you accept that you're worthy, you will feel more confident and you just might find that you're a better wife and a better mother—you're going to be a better you, a complete turnaround. Your self-esteem and worth permeate every area of your being, as well as how you operate in the world. When I got to the point where I believed the words I repeated, I started to work on the rest of it: clothes, makeup, and even sex.

The "Love On" Campaign

When the benefits of the internal work became apparent, I decided that my outside should reflect my newfound confidence. So I launched my "love on" campaign, where I selected something about me that I thought was flawed and found a reason to love it.

Before addressing my perceived flaws, I started with something I already appreciated: my eyes. I have always found beauty in my eyes. I love that my eyes are almondy. (If you don't get that reference, we can't be friends!) Keeping it 100, this was back in the day when I watched *Keeping Up with the Kardashians,* and I heard Robert tell his girls that if they're going to be getting into makeup, they were going to know how to do it right so they didn't look a mess. He hired a professional makeup artist to teach them. That seemed like sound advice to me. If I was going to do this, I wanted to do it right. I found professional help in the form of YouTube makeup gurus and their step-by-step tutorials. I was all in! I watched, learned, experimented, and watched some more. With my budding confidence and my dedication to "love on" my eyes, I decided to introduce makeup into my daily life. I went to my nearest MAC store and bought Woodwinked and Amber Lights eyeshadow. There was something special about feeling good on the inside and allowing that feeling to sparkle brightly on the outside.

Once I had fully embraced the love I had for my eyes, I moved on to the parts of me where I needed more convincing. I never liked my legs, which I thought were scrawny and unsexy. When women emulated—and men swooned over—a quintessential "Black body," it always seemed to mean thick, curvy, and busty. I was none of those things. To "love on" my legs, I had to reconcile what the world seemed to love about Black women's bodies. I started wearing miniskirts and short shorts to showcase those legs.

Sometimes we need to renew how we think about ourselves, taking the time to focus on the characteristics we like. We all have things we would change if we could, but we can't. It's best to learn to love those things, because no good comes from hating them. We are all flawed. Stop looking in the mirror and focusing on the flaws, and stop thinking they're the most important part of you. No one notices your flaws the way you do. I promise. I want you to tell yourself that until you believe it.

I'm going to get a little churchy here. In all my Bible study, I learned that God made us in his image, and we are all *fearfully and wonderfully made*.[1] In other words, people are all uniquely designed as separate individuals, and God thinks of all of us as his masterpieces. He loves everything about me, so I should love all my parts too. Every one of our features was put here intentionally. With that line of thinking, if God created me as a masterpiece, why don't I like my skin or my cheekbones or my hair? I should be proud of the traits that are mine and take the time to make them shine. That is why I encourage you to find something that you like about yourself and love on it. Focus on it. Emphasize it. Give it all the love you have.

The "Make Me Over" Campaign

In my late twenties, I was obsessed with a TV series called *What Not to Wear*. On the show, people were instructed to buy different sets of clothes for work, for going out at night, for church, and for hanging out around the house. The idea was to have a wardrobe that could transition no matter the occasion. The choices in my closet didn't work like that. One time, Kevin and I were getting ready to go out, just the two of us. I wanted to get dressed up for date night with my husband, but I had only church clothes and work clothes, none of which I wanted to wear on my night out. To paint the picture, I worked as an assistant manager of a bank. If it's been a minute since you've walked into your local branch, let me describe my wardrobe: buttoned-up collared shirts, black or gray slacks, and flat Steve Madden kitten heels or mules.

I didn't want to feel like a career girl or a church lady on a date with my husband, but I had nothing in my closet that I could even finesse to be date wear. I felt dowdy and boring. That occasion forced me to take inventory. I wanted to feel my best going on a date with my husband or even running to CVS on a Saturday afternoon. So I paid more attention to *What Not to Wear,* figuring out what clothes worked best for my body type, what I liked and didn't like on me, and what risks I was willing to take.

As women, we take on many roles: wife, mother, daughter, sister, employee, boss, friend. We tend to forget what it means to fully assume the role of being a woman. It's easy to forget the importance of taking pride in ourselves. Far too many times, I have walked out of the house looking a hot mess and feeling even worse. You know what I'm talking about. It's when you're out and you say a silent prayer that you don't run into anyone you know because you're hating your hair, your makeup, your clothes. You don't want to feel embarrassed about your appearance. No one wants to feel like that.

Now, of course, we all have days where we just don't have it in us to get ourselves together. Chile, I have days like that all the time. But even on those days, I try to make the minimum effort. I'm mostly talking about the times when you know you could have done more but didn't. I want you to walk out of the house hoping to see someone and to have yourself be seen.

To be clear, I walk tall *not* because of what my husband, my kids, or other people think and say but because I know that I feel better when I make an effort. I do it for me. You're worth the time and effort it takes to walk tall. And you should do it for you.

The "Sex Me Over" Campaign

After putting in the work on my self-esteem, I took my campaigns to the bedroom. For me, there had always been two huge obstacles keeping me from feeling sexy. The first was that I didn't find anything sexy about my appearance. The second is that I was never taught to acknowledge, let alone embrace, my sexuality. Quite the opposite, in fact. I was taught to tamp down anything that might be evocative of sex. The word *sexy* was nowhere in my brain, in my vocabulary, in my world. Therefore, the word *sexy* did not find its way into my closet.

Back when I was looking to give myself a makeover, I was watching a YouTube video, and the fashion expert was talking about "sexy boots for the fall and winter." She held up a rockin' pair of thigh-high boots. My mind raced. Not only had I never put on a pair of thigh-high boots, but I had never described anything that I owned or wanted to own as sexy.

Those boots turned a lightbulb on in my head: How was it that I, a married woman with two kids (living proof that I had had sex), never in my life felt sexy? How had I never allowed myself to use that word in reference to me? It's not that I needed those boots, per se, but I needed to feel that I was sexy. God created me to be a sexual being. It was time for me to embrace it and own it.

The "sex me over" campaign was my personal quest to accept that I'm a sexy, sexual woman. In the early years of my marriage, I remember purchasing lingerie, putting it on, and immediately feeling insecure about it. I worried that Kevin would notice the areas I wished I could hide or change (of course he wouldn't), and my insecurity took me out of the moment. I realized that I needed to take a "fake it till you make it" approach. I started to initiate sex. I reminded myself that it's okay to want sex, to desire touch—things that were forbidden for most of my life. And though it wasn't like my insecurities around sex melted away as soon as I started doing these things, I came to see that there was power in acting like a sexual being.

Confidence shines through your pores and actually serves to make you more appealing to others. If you have more confidence in your appearance, you're going to have more confidence in the bedroom, and your marriage will benefit from your new-found sense of self. I have learned that sex is for me. Now when I buy lingerie, I focus on how it makes *me* feel, 'cause that's what matters! When I take a shower, use body wash, or put on perfume, I turn myself on. *I smell good, my legs are glistening, I've got this little nightie on—I'm poppin'! I'm feeling myself tonight!* I do it for me.

When I turned thirty, less than a year after I started "sexing myself over," I read the book *The Good Girl's Guide to Great Sex* by Sheila Wray Gregoire. It convinced me to take more risks with respect to my role as a sexual married woman. As such, I created an alter ego named Sin-ammon, who was born when I went on a sisters' weekend in Vegas. My sisters and I were determined to have good, clean fun. But they are far more risqué than I am, so when they suggested a pole-dancing class, I was super hesitant and, frankly, a little embarrassed. I didn't want to dance on a pole in front of a bunch of strangers. But I did it, and it was a huge moment for me. I learned a few moves and had a blast. It was the first time I let myself explore that side of myself publicly. It was liberating.

Sin-ammon allows me to lose the inhibitions that Melissa has always been burdened by. I'm low-key conservative, but Sin-ammon allows me to get freaky. I now get my lingerie from Savage X Fenty by Rihanna, which is next level. (Y'all know

Rihanna don't play no games.) My confidence was the engine that took me from one end of the sexual spectrum to the other.

Feeling like a sexy person can exist separately from dressing sexy and having sex. So much of sex and sexuality is connected to confidence. In a way, the clothes are irrelevant. You can be fully clothed and be sexy—it's how you view and carry yourself.

Compare and Despair

To people who listen to our podcasts or follow me on social media, it may look like I have it all together. I promise you I do not. I don't want anyone looking at me or my family and thinking, *I need to get where she is.* I don't want anyone thinking about their own life in comparison to what they think I am.

Comparison and competition are the thieves of self-esteem and confidence. When I compare who I am and what I have with what you are and what you have, I will never be happy with me. It's cliché but worth stating: People post only their best days on social media. I don't post any selfies if my hair isn't done. That's just the facts. I have bad hair days. Plenty of them. They just don't make it to my Instagram feed.

As I said earlier, I had to consciously shift my standard of beauty in order for it to include myself. So, I advise you to become your own standard of beauty. It's great to be inspired by other people, as long as it's a healthy inspiration. Just don't compare yourselves to others in a way that leads you to envy them and thus reject who you are. My self-esteem cannot be contingent on others. I am in competition only with myself to be better than I was yesterday. I mean, seriously, why would I compare myself to Halle Berry when I'm never going to be her?

This may be hard to believe, but the beauty you see in others is the same beauty others see in you. What I mean is, others are likely noticing beautiful things about you that you don't see in yourself. Even now, if I get compliments about my appearance, it jars me. I remember going on tour and being shocked when people came up to me and said, "You're so much prettier in person." (Still not sure that was a genuine compliment, since it might have just meant my social media photos were subpar, but let's go with it.) The reaction didn't equate with how I viewed myself. We tend to judge ourselves much more critically than we judge others. We tend to think that everyone else is happier, is prettier, and has something we need. I promise you, someone is looking at you wishing they had what you have, wishing they looked like you, wishing they were more like you. This is why your self-esteem cannot be dictated by other people. Other people are finicky, but you should always be able to count on yourself. I've learned that I can count on my inner monologue to remind me that I am worth it.

I Am the Reason and the Occasion

In the midst of all these campaigns, I got dressed up one day—not because I had anywhere special to be but because I was feeling good and I had the confidence to put myself together. On my way out the door, I ran into a neighbor who took a long look at me and said, "Where you going today? What you got going on?" My response was "I am the reason and the occasion."

At the root of this mantra is an affirmation of worthiness. I created it to give myself permission to be extra, to celebrate me for no reason other than me. And to do it without guilt or shame. How many times have you saved a cute outfit, waiting for the perfect occasion? It sits there with the tags, waiting for you to do that outfit the favor of wearing it. *You* are the reason. *You* are the occasion.

Think of yourself as a piece of jewelry. You are not a two-dollar ring that someone picked up at the drugstore, a trinket that is easily replaceable. You are more like a Tiffany ring—and that ring goes in a velvet box, doesn't it? You are worth the velveted blue box with the white ribbon. You are not a piece of discount costume junk that should be thrown in the bottom of the drawer. We think we're not worth it. Well, I am worth it, and so are you.

I don't want you to think for a fraction of a second that I'm suggesting that feeling good about yourself can come from going shopping. Quite the contrary, in fact. When I say that you're worth putting on a nice outfit and doing your hair, I mean you should know that you deserve it, even on days when you decide to keep it casual. Self-esteem is not attained by acquiring stuff. No amount of clothing or makeup or plastic surgery is going to give you self-worth, and you can't make up for low self-esteem by putting on designer labels, wearing makeup, or injecting your face with fillers. When it all comes off, you have to be comfortable with who you are.

You are like a diamond. Yes, there are ways to measure a diamond: weight, clarity, flawlessness. But any diamond has intrinsic value simply because it's a diamond. I tell myself, *Simply because I am, I am worthy.* Just *being* makes me valuable—makes you valuable. I get dressed and do my hair simply because this makes me feel good about myself. I don't need another reason. And you don't either!

Relationship Check-In

(For your relationship with yourself):

- How do you talk to yourself?

Do you keep it positive?

"I'm worth it, as is, without change, without exception."
"I deserve to be in every room I find myself in."
"I am worthy of love."

Or is your self-talk negative?

"I wish I could change____"
"I hate my____"
"If only I were more like____"

- What is the tone of your inner monologue?
- Are you your biggest fan, or are you your biggest critic?
- When was the last time you said or did something kind for yourself?
- For men and women whose partners might be dealing with low self-esteem or self-worth, you can support them with words of affirmation and encouragement: What do you admire most about your partner? When was the last time you told them that?

Chapter Twelve

Lessons from Eighteen Years of Marriage

Every year, on or around our anniversary, we do a podcast talking about the lessons we've learned in the previous twelve months. Over the course of four seasons and fifty-two weeks, couples go through countless experiences and challenges that force them to evolve. An anniversary is not just another day; it's a day that matters. You've made it another year together. It's a time to celebrate and also a time to take stock.

We're ending the book with our most valued lessons from eighteen years of marriage. The ending of this book is also a beginning for you. In your marriage, each day you spend together informs the next day. We think there are two perfect annual occasions to reflect on the lessons you're learning: your anniversary and/or the end of the calendar year. We suggest making the time to take inventory and set an intention as you go into a new year.

The fifteen lessons we list in this chapter are not mutually exclusive—they bump into each other, complement each other, support each other. The way we experience these lessons is in layers that build on and around each other, forming the narrative and shared understanding of our relationship.

Lesson #1: Resentment

Melissa:

Our first lesson is a recent one. We learned it in 2020 during quarantine, when we were forced to deal with the resentment we'd been holding in for years.

I define *resentment* as "unvoiced anger." It is often a silent relationship killer, like a smoldering fire that doesn't get extinguished. When you're in a marriage, it's not easy to be aware of the resentment building unless you make an active choice to pay attention to it. Resentment is extremely dangerous in relationships because it intensifies with time and erodes your emotional connection with your partner. It's no longer about the behavior that made you mad; it is *them*. That is how divorce starts. Instead of thinking, *Our relationship needs help and attention and focus,* it becomes about the other person's character. *All these problems are the result of* you *being in my life. If I get you out, I will have peace.* Sitting in that narrative is dangerous.

We've talked about resentment more than once throughout this book. When Kev and I each used the words "Get out of my car," we failed to be empathic to the other, and it led to resentment. When we lost our dream house, I felt abandoned, lonely, and isolated. I started to recall all the times when Kevin "made" me feel this way, and I became indignant and even more settled in my anger. The narrative in my head was that he never showed up for me or my feelings. I couldn't allow myself to give more than I felt I was getting. I started to be stingy with my feelings. I held back both emotionally and physically. And so begins the cycle of resentment.

I've found it's so much more productive to take an empathic

stance toward Kevin. When he's doing things that make me crazy, I do my best to understand where he's coming from. I try to make sense of the situation from his perspective. Once you step into your partner's shoes, there's a good chance the resentment will fade. If I can empathize with what you're thinking, feeling, or experiencing, it becomes a connection point, even in the midst of conflict. At the end of the day, empathy is what connects people. Once the empathy is severed, you might as well be enemies.

The longer you're in a relationship, the more likely you are to have a case file of times you've been wronged by your partner. Longevity gives resentment an opportunity to build up, and if you sit with those feelings, the resentment remains on fertile ground, growing and festering. Your history prevents you from giving your spouse a clean slate, and even when you're trying to have empathy for them, issues from your past can still be triggered. This was especially true for me during quarantine, when I stewed in feeling unappreciated and left out of important decisions; it all came to the surface as resentment. I had to be careful about the narrative I was repeating to myself about those wrongdoings.

Identifying resentment in your relationship takes some reflection, but here are a few examples of how resentment can manifest itself:

1. Being angry or short-tempered
2. Lacking empathy or being unwilling to see your partner's point of view
3. Focusing on the bad parts of your relationship
4. Criticizing your partner's character
5. Engaging in tit-for-tat behavior or scorekeeping
6. Withdrawing emotionally and/or sexually
7. Blaming your spouse without taking accountability

The first step to reclaiming your relationship is identifying the fact that you are harboring feelings of resentment. The second is communicating those feelings, and the third is getting professional help from a couples counselor.

Kevin:

I'm no counselor, but I've been married for a long periolodical (*sic*) time, and what I know for sure is that resentment is real! I have to be very diligent with my thoughts to ensure I'm not allowing room for resentment to build. The dangerous part of resentment is that it's not overt. It's a feeling that creates a bucket in your mind. When your spouse says and does things that hurt you or irritate you, you put it all in the same bucket. For instance, your partner is late to pick you up and you think, *She's not late because of traffic or being held up at work; she's late because she is inconsiderate and just doesn't care about me.* You've got to get to the root of what is bugging you and deal with that head-on. Cut the resentment off at the pass. Don't give it a chance to live rent-free in your head and do damage to your marriage.

Lull Mengesha, a good friend of mine from college, gave some good advice. He said, "Approach every situation as if the person you are interacting with has the best intentions." Even if it's not always true, that framing often helps us see the good in people, giving them the benefit of the doubt. With your spouse, it is extremely helpful. Your mind follows whichever narrative you let lead, so if resentment is unchallenged, it will lead. If you lead with best intentions, your mind will frame the situation that way.

Lesson #2: Differentiation

Melissa:

Y'all know I love a good definition, so here is mine for *differentiation:* "the act of setting goals that are just for you." These are things you want to do that have nothing to do with your spouse, kids, mama, daddy, pastor, first lady . . . basically everyone and everybody else! It's crucial that you feel recognized outside the roles you play at home.

I'm going to speak to you women for a second. Many of you find that your greatest purpose in life is being a mother. I get it. Your children are your whole heart. They are the most important thing in the world. But they are going to grow up. They are going to be independent, autonomous people who will leave your house to have their own lives. They are a season—a long season, but a season nonetheless.

I mean no disrespect or shame here, but part of growing into a relationship is recognizing that you are an individual. It's essential that you show up in the world as your authentic self and stay in tune with your needs, wants, desires, goals, and ambitions. It's crucial that you have an understanding of, and a relationship with, yourself. You might fear that if you spend time investing in hobbies or activities that are separate from your partner, you'll hurt your connection with them, but people in a relationship do not need to be consumed with every single aspect of each other's world. Sacrificing your desires is dangerous, because it leaves room for resentment to grow (see Lesson #1). Everyone needs their own identities and times in the day or week or month that are just for them.

To be clear, I'm not talking about something that brings in

money. I'm talking about finding out what fulfills you beyond the role that you took on when you said "I do" or became a parent. Read a romance novel, take a painting class, do sunrise yoga, or learn to speak French. Being differentiated doesn't mean you lose connection with your spouse or your kids. In fact, it helps you connect with them better, because you know who you are and can show up more authentically.

Keeping it 100, I was never the super spontaneous friend, even as a teenager. I was always down for a good time, but when my friends got together, I usually acted as the responsible one, the one who could call our parents for help in the event the night's shenanigans went awry. And as wife and mother, I was even less fun and spontaneous. I leaned into routine and predictability. I forgot how much I enjoyed going out with friends, trying new food and restaurants, and being a tourist in my own town. I had to learn how to do things that felt good to me.

Years ago, I was about to take a five-day trip for work that included a weekend. Someone said to me right before I left town, "Oh, I could never be away from my kids that long." It gave me pause. Was I supposed to feel a certain way about leaving my kids? I felt guilty that I'd planned the whole trip without feeling that concern. And for a moment, I considered canceling, which was crazy. Y'all, my kids were going to be well taken care of. Their daddy would be home the whole time.

It made me realize that when we sacrifice something "for our kids," it's often something our kids don't even want or need. We make that sacrifice because other parents expect us to. It's that mommy shaming, and it is real!

Kevin:

As Melissa says, life with children at home is a season. That hit me when we started going out and leaving our kids at home alone. It began with a quick trip to 7-Eleven, just to give the boys a chance to get used to it. They were eight and ten at the time, and it was silly how much we worried about driving half a mile away and being gone for ten minutes. But soon, Melissa and I worked up to having lunch at the mall on weekends, and I gotta tell you, it was freeing! Next thing we knew, we were going to dinner, and when we got home, the boys had already gone to bed on their own. It felt like we were back in college. We could go out for a drink and not have to worry. I felt young again.

I used to lie to myself by saying that I do stand-up comedy for my kids. Yes, providing for my wife and kids has been *one* of the benefits of taking this career path. But it's not why I do it. I do it because I love it. A great benefit of being successful at something I love is that my family likely will not have to worry about finances, but that's not what made me take it on originally. I did it for *me*. And it involves sacrifices: I'm not at every soccer game; I'm not at every practice; I'm not at last-minute school events.

Now that the kids are older, I notice my role shifting. It's a huge change from the years when they were infants and couldn't even hold their heads up, change themselves, or eat without us cooking for them. They don't need us like that anymore. When I first dropped Isaiah off at kindergarten, he just walked right in. I was shocked! He never looked back. That independence brought tears to my eyes. Now that he's in high school, he hardly needs us at all. He orders his food on Postmates, cooks his own meals, wakes up on his own, and goes to bed on his own. If he had his own money, he wouldn't need us at all. As a matter of fact, the only text messages he responds to are when he asks us for games on his phone and needs our approval.

I've worked to find ways to give my kids what really matters to them, and those things are different for each kid. My younger son needs quality time; that's his love language. What that looks like is playing video games together, specifically the games he likes. Right now he loves a game called Spelunky, which is incredibly difficult for a man my age. When he asks me to play and I'm super busy, I try to at least play with him for thirty minutes. Our older son loves movies, so he and I see basically every Marvel film and action movie in existence.

As parents, we often feel like we don't have time for the activities with our kids, but as Gay Hendricks explains, the fact is that we don't *make* the time. If your kid came to you while you were busy working and said, "Can you play video games with me?" you would say, "I'm sorry, I don't have time." But if they fell and broke their leg or had a nosebleed, you would make the time. You have the time in both instances, but on one occasion you decide it's important enough to stop what you're doing. To be great parents, you have to make time for all of it.

Melissa and I look back fondly on our high school and college days, thinking, *We did everything together.* The truth is we did a lot together, but there were certain things we did separately. I studied acting; Melissa studied law. It was good that we could bring different interests and subjects to the table. You gotta do some things on your own. It's important to have hobbies that occupy your alone time. (Side note: The best thing I do on my own is masturbation, because it's something that I can do for myself that makes me feel good.)

Lesson #3: Seasons

Melissa:

As you've heard me say countless times, marriage has seasons, and different circumstances will bring on changes in your relationship. When my parents got divorced, my emotional reaction brought on a new season between me and Kev. If your extended family presents problems, that can transport you from one season to another.

There are four seasons in a year, and each season requires different clothing. You won't be wearing your winter coat in summer or your tank tops and shorts in the winter. In the same way, we should also consider the change of seasons in our relationships. What do we need to keep, purge, or stow away? What is no longer applicable or necessary? What can we use to grow in the coming season? You can approach these conversations with something Kevin and I learned in corporate America called the Stop, Start, Continue method. What do you want to stop? What do you want to start? What do you want to continue?

If you're not staying on top of that, you're going to bring old (or bad) habits into the next season, and they will no longer suit you. Just as you want to leave the bad stuff behind, you want to make sure you're not also leaving the good stuff in the past season as you continue on.

One of my biggest life regrets is a decision I made based on information from an old season in our marriage. When Kevin asked me to join him on tour back in 2018, our dynamic was that I acted as the responsible adult in our relationship and Kevin was the dreamer. Kevin had this brilliant idea to self-produce and finance a national and international tour, and he wanted us to do it together—he wanted me to leave my job and go out on a limb and chase dreams with him. I didn't do it. I couldn't do it. I was afraid. I was afraid that if this didn't work, we would be left without the safety net of my corporate job.

While I thought I was making a good decision for my family at the time—and to some degree I still believe I was—I also believe that it came at a cost to my marriage: the cost of partnership. The tour worked, and suddenly we were in a different season of life. It's not easy for me to say I was wrong, but I was. Completely wrong. It is one of my biggest marriage regrets. The importance of recognizing the moment, the season, is something that we are still rectifying to this day.

While I was eventually given a second chance, that doesn't mean it came without consequences. It's kinda like wearing shorts in the winter and getting frostbite. Did you die? No! But you're sure going to miss that pinkie toe. For us, those consequences included Kevin not feeling like I was on his side, which ultimately sent him on a search for a new teammate, making me feel like even more of an outsider. We've been working together only since 2018, and it wasn't until quarantine in 2020 that these issues were vocalized. By the summer of 2021, we finally began the process of healing those traumas through therapy and communication.

As the seasons in your marriage change, so will your responsibilities and needs. Be flexible, agile, and sensitive enough to grow, evolve, and pivot accordingly. If you don't, you'll be holding on to a mindset that no longer suits, serves, or fits your marriage.

Kevin:

Last year, we went to a vineyard in Napa, and the sommelier was talking about this one type of wine. He explained that because of the bad weather that year, the entire vintage was affected, making the wine acidic. For another vintage, the region had wildfires, and the wine from that year has some smokiness as a result. It doesn't mean every bottle of wine from that vineyard is bad or tainted or smoky. But some years have rough patches, and the wine shows it. Marriages are the same. You don't throw the bad season away. You take what you learned from it and move on. You can use it to prepare for the next season.

Lesson #4: Vulnerability

Melissa:

In her song "Giving You the Best That I Got," Anita Baker sings, "I bet everything on my wedding ring."[1] I loooove this line. I take it to mean "No one else believes in us, and I am still choosing you." I feel like I did this with Kevin. In Washington, I had a job at Boeing and was making good money; we had a house, and my kids were in private school. Yet I picked up and moved to Los Angeles to help my man chase his dream.

Still, I've wondered, *What does it mean to "bet everything" on your marriage?* In poker, when a player is all in, they have put the last of their chips into the pot. As a result, they cannot perform another action. It is the ultimate bet and the ultimate gamble. Have I really bet everything on my wedding ring? Have I truly been vulnerable enough to share *everything*? When I think back on it, my answer is no.

As I've gotten older, I realize that vulnerability is what establishes connection and longevity in relationships. It's the glue that keeps you together, because you're sharing pieces of yourself that no one else has access to but your partner. You expose yourself to them in a way you don't with anyone else. It is the foundation of trust, intimacy, and connection. Without it, there is a certain shallowness to your relationship that is hard to overcome.

Kevin:

Everyone brings baggage from previous relationships into the next ones. If we were previously lied to, cheated on, or mistreated, we're going to avoid being vulnerable in the future. It's how we protect ourselves from revisiting that pain.

When we can't sleep, Melissa and I often have tough conversations that lead to deep revelations. One time, she pointed out to me that I was really good at sharing my dreams and hopes and plans but that I never shared my fears. She said that our conversations weren't deep enough, but what she really meant was that she was missing out on my vulnerability.

She was right. I did some self-work and realized that I avoided acknowledging my fears because I thought voicing them would make them turn into realities. I learned that I'm not going to add realness to something by acknowledging it. It's going to either happen or not happen, whether or not I've shared my fears with my wife. Getting vulnerable was not going to hurt me. If anything, sharing my fears with Melissa helps me manage them and put them to bed. But I'm not going to lie; it was hard at first.

At first I struggled with figuring out what to even share. To be honest, I was afraid, so I just unloaded everything that was making me anxious.

"At work, somebody may have gone to HR on me."

"What if my next comedy set isn't on par with the old ones?"

"What if I don't make it?"

Melissa knew I was trying, so she applauded my effort, and it allowed me to continue down the path. Words of affirmation are my love language, and her encouragement and appreciation have helped me get better at being vulnerable. When I started therapy, I learned more about sharing vulnerabilities. The more I went, the more I understood my fears and got better at connecting with Melissa about them.

Lesson #5: Sex

Melissa:

Sex. Have it. Prioritize it.

Kevin:

This is a short segment. Sex can be short sometimes.

One lesson that I have learned is that sometimes sex just needs to feel good. That's it. No other requirements. Early in my marriage, my ego got in the way (as it did in many aspects of my relationship with Melissa). I felt that if Melissa didn't finish, I had failed. I approached every session as a task that needed to be completed. It was all or nothing. If she didn't climax, I was a terrible husband. So I just kept going: Keep licking, keep licking, to infinity and beyond!

I needed to see the physical response. Every time. But that ended up putting pressure on her. Melissa had to shed some light: "I don't have to finish in order for it to feel good." Just like you don't have to clean your plate to enjoy your meal. You can eat three ribs off a rack, and they'll taste delicious. Over time, I learned to enjoy the moment without putting pressure on us. I was able to relax without going to my usual, *If this sex sucks, then I suck. I'm a terrible lover, so she'll find someone who makes her climax every time, and she'll leave me for him.*

To be honest, removing that pressure has led to better experiences in the bedroom. As soon as I stopped thinking about sex as something that had to be done to completion, it allowed for more enjoyment of the experience.

Lesson #6: Experience Firsts Together

Melissa:

When you're in a relationship, you're in the memory-making business. One of the best ways to bond with your partner is to experience firsts together. Jet Ski, parasail, travel internationally, make chocolate—do these things for the first time together. They might not go well, but even bad experiences make for important memories. If I eat something that tastes terrible, I want everyone at the table to eat it too. Why? Because it's a memory, a bond, a connection that'll forever tie us to each other.

One of the best firsts Kev and I experienced was actually a two-parter. As we wrote earlier, we had a grand total of $384 to spend on our entire honeymoon. On that trip, we were fool enough to walk into a Ruth's Chris Steak House in San Francisco to have dinner. We sat down in a plush red leather booth, got some water, and looked at the menu. Chile, there was not a single thing that we could afford. Not even a side dish. We had no business being there.

Kevin:

Before our honeymoon, the most expensive restaurant we had been to was Red Lobster on prom night. (For the record, Melissa got the Admiral's Feast for $22.99.) At Ruth's Chris, I saw that the least expensive entrée was the $36 stuffed chicken breast. We figured we would order two chicken breasts and asked the waitress what it came with. "It's à la carte," she said. I didn't speak French, with the exception of à la mode. She explained that the sides were $11 or $12 each. I did the math in my head and came to the conclusion that if we ordered dinner, we would live in Ruth's Chris, because there would be no money left for the cab back to the hotel.

I asked the waitress to give us a few minutes to decide what we wanted. When she walked away, I turned to Liss. "We can't afford to eat here," I said. When no one was looking, we made an exit through the kitchen, down an alley, and around the corner to a burger joint where we got two cheeseburgers for $11.

In the moment, we were embarrassed. It was mortifying that we couldn't afford the steak dinner. We worried that we'd done a version of a dine and dash, but it was more like a look and dash. Now, though, we think back on that night as a fun memory. That desperate escape is something we will never forget. We were dead broke, but we were in it together—and that was the whole point.

Like Melissa said, this story has a second part: the first time we actually ate at Ruth's Chris, for our ten-year anniversary. By that point, the meal was still an extravagance, but it wasn't going to break us. We got the lobster mac and cheese, the garlic mashed potatoes, the cowboy rib eye, and a bottle of Chianti. I think everything tasted better simply because of what happened the first time we entered a Ruth's Chris. We appreciated every morsel of food and drop of wine in a way we wouldn't have without that look and dash.

Another great memory was the first time we took the boys to Paris. We were walking from the Champs-Élysées on our way to the Louvre, and midway through our walk in the Tuileries Garden, we came upon a broken-down old carnival. The kids' eyes lit up, and they begged us to take them in. I'm thinking, *Really? I'm missing the* Mona Lisa *for this junk?* The boys went on a ragged ride (I swear it looked like it came out of a suitcase), and we never even made it to the museum. Here, we thought we were going to see the *Mona Lisa,* but instead we were at a stupid haunted house. And the thing is, the boys had the time of their lives at that sketchy fair. I had had one idea of what would be fun, and the boys had another. The takeaway is that sometimes you gotta just let the moment be the moment, as opposed to what you thought the moment was going to be. *C'est la vie!*

Lesson #7: Parenthood

Melissa:

The lesson here is simple: Child-rearing lasts for a season; your marriage lasts for a lifetime. Actively prioritize your marriage even while your children are young. Dream together; develop goals together. Remember your partner and the reasons you fell in love. When your kids leave home, it'll be just the two of you again. Make sure when that time comes, you're not looking at a stranger.

As we discussed in chapter 5, "Marital Roles Be Hard," for Kevin and me, becoming parents affected us in a way we didn't anticipate beforehand or even realize in real time. We went from doing everything together as a couple to splitting off, because I stayed home with the boys while Kevin went to clubs at night to pursue his dream. To be clear, I was never a SAHM (stay-at-home mom), but when Kevin was out doing shows that I would have attended in a previous season, I now stayed home with the boys since we didn't always have money for a babysitter.

Shortly before we sat down to write this book, Kev and I addressed the fact that we just don't know how to work well together. When we look back, we realize that it started when we had kids. He was busy making dreams come true, and I was working a traditional job during the day and staying home in the evenings with the boys. I wish we had done things differently. I wish we were more intentional about maintaining our relationship. We are just now at a point of bridging the gap that formed almost fifteen years ago.

Kevin:

The Bible says, "Train up a child in the way that he should go."[2] Because he got to go! You're training them to leave you. Our job as parents is for those boys to need us less and less every day. I need them to leave so Melissa and I can go to Bora Bora. Because we don't want to go with the boys. They messed up Spain by asking how to get on the Wi-Fi, and I will never forgive them for that.

Lesson #8: Marriage Be Hard

Melissa:

I used to *hate* when people said to me, "Marriage is so much work!" It made marriage seem undesirable, and it didn't seem to describe Kevin's and my relationship. After eighteen years, though? Let me tell you: Marriage be hard! There are days, even years, when we're vibing really well. But other days (or years) take a lot of work. Most of that work is internal, where you deal with your own triggers and insecurities and mess-ups and ways you show up in your relationship. Marriage is an exercise in selflessness, and you cannot be selfless unless you first learn what you're all about.

A true indicator of a healthy relationship is not the absence of conflict but the presence of conflict resolution. How you work through the challenges is most important. When my marriage is in a challenging season, here are some tips that I call up:

- My partner is my teammate, not my enemy.
- Therapy helps. Go to it, both alone and as a couple.
- Cultivate intimacy (physical and emotional).
- If you put in the work, the good will outweigh the bad.

Kevin:

Yes, marriage is hard, but when you approach the hard work together, you win. I win mostly because Melissa tells me where to put in the work. She pinpoints our weaknesses and identifies the paths, processes, and conversations that will make us stronger. She is my cheat sheet.

The irony is that when you own and cultivate and manage the "marriage be hard" lesson, it frees things up for the two of you, making marriage easier than it might otherwise be.

Lesson #9: Honor

Melissa:

To honor your partner means to esteem, encourage, and acknowledge them for the work they do. A simple thank-you goes a long way toward making your partner feel honored. And to be brutally honest, I'm terrible at it. As far as love languages go, words of affirmation are actually pretty low on my list. That does not mean I don't need to feel appreciated. I do, and so does my husband. When you articulate why you admire your spouse, it ensures they don't feel taken for granted.

In that spirit, I want to publicly honor Kevin for the following things:

- As a father: I know you always jokingly brag about how you're a great father, but you truly are. The way you interact with the boys and show up for them is beautiful to witness.
- As a husband: With each year, I recognize that your love for me runs deep. Even when I'm on your nerves (which is never, because I don't get on nerves, right?), you always move toward reconciliation. And you do it even when I want to be mad longer. I love you for that.
- As a businessman: I don't think folks really understand how business savvy you are. There is something in the way that you're wired that you just get it, and it's special.

You are so much more than Instagram videos and funny skits. Your work ethic, drive, determination, and motivation make you the hardest-working man on the internet. When people ask me who inspires me, I always say, "My husband."

I love you, Kevin. I honor you. I appreciate all that you are.

Kevin:

Thank you for that, Melissa. I *am* a great father. I am glad you, and now the world, can appreciate my triumphs in that area.

Now it's my turn.

- As a mother: You truly are the world's best mother. You are kind enough to take on the role of being the bad guy with the kids almost all the time. The boys are well behaved because you demand it of them. You take them to school, pick them up, do the math and art projects, cut their nails, and take them to soccer. All I do is play video games with them and say, "Boys, take the trash down and bring it back up." I am super weak for that. But thank you.

- As a wife: You are a gift from God. Point-blank. Period. You consider my feelings before your own. I honestly don't want you doing that, but you do it anyway. You will make sure I am good even if it means you aren't.

  Your self-reflection is also wildly impressive. You are on a constant search to be the best version of yourself, and I admire that. You are relentless. You read books, listen to podcasts, watch TED Talks—you name it! Then, you take what you learned and apply it to our lives. You don't just let it wash over; you do the real work. You share information and lessons with me, and by default, I become better as well. You have the best intentions, and you don't let yourself off the hook. It inspires me to follow in your wake and do the hard work as well.

- As an entrepreneur: I am glad you are embracing your creativity. You have a wealth of amazing ideas, you have a knack for development, and you know when something works. You have helped me make so many things better, and I'm excited to see what you develop and produce on your own. With my support, of course.

Lesson #10: Spontaneity

Melissa:

One Friday recently, Kevin expressed that he wanted to have a really chill weekend. We decided to take a little staycation at a hotel about forty minutes away from our house. When we arrived at the hotel, Kevin asked me, "Why did you say yes to coming when you have a ton of work to do?"

I replied, "I usually feel like I need to be the no to your yes. I just wanted to be spontaneous with you today."

We had a great weekend together. It was relaxing, but more important to me, it was spontaneous.

Adulthood is often boring and predictable. And if romance involves novelty, it follows that boredom is the antithesis of romance. You have to mix it up. Spontaneity is the cure for those ruts and doldrums. Admittedly, I'm not the best at flying by the seat of my pants, and I worry that I'm less fun now than I used to be before kids and work and responsibilities. But it's important to still feel like the girlfriend even when you're the wife. I am promising myself a little more fun and spontaneity in our future.

Kevin:

I must say, that weekend away was so fantastic. Same city, completely different vibe. It brought me back to our college days, when we would go to IHOP for pancakes in the middle of the night. Those were good times, and we don't have that kind of flexibility anymore. Our whole life is planned, but we still want to feel young and fun and spontaneous and carefree and sometimes irresponsible. When Melissa was willing to pick up and head to that hotel spontaneously, it brought back the feelings I had when we were young, stupid kids, and I loved it.

Early in our marriage, I never would have asked Melissa for a spontaneous getaway. And I have to say, I was a little surprised when she said yes without hesitation. I was expecting her to say no. In fact, I wouldn't even have been upset, because we both had work to do. (We always have work to do.) When she said yes, I sprang into action. It showed me that she does the work: She learns what's good for a relationship and uses what she learns to make our marriage better.

Lesson #11: Dream Together

Melissa:

Truthfully, I've never been a dreamer. Like, ever. Even as a child, my dreams were always grounded by what I thought was possible and reasonable.

On *The Love Hour*, one of our listeners described a kite-

and-string dynamic that often exists in relationships. The kite appears to be the more interesting person of the pair—the colorful thing that soars through the sky. When you see a kite flying through the air, you watch the kite, not the person holding the string. String holders do the things that don't get noticed. String holders show up consistently. Kites cannot fly unless someone is holding the string.

In our relationship, I am without question the string holder. I am the person grounded by reality. I take the safe route. When we're making big decisions, I am careful, practical. I think about safety nets and protection plans.

Being married to a kite has taught me the value of dreaming. I still believe in grounding dreams with a plan, but I have also learned the value of releasing yourself from reality for a moment and seeing an alternate future in which you never fail. What risks would you take if you weren't terrified of failure? It's still a work in progress for me, but it is something I practice more and more.

Dreaming together is a very intimate experience. It allows you to share your wildest desires and innermost aspirations with your partner and then ask them to come along for the ride.

Kevin:

Melissa has been the string to my kite, but I don't view that negatively. It's crucial to have a string to keep us kites from flying away and getting tangled in a tree. When I wanted to move to Los Angeles and thought it would be a good idea to let our house in Washington go into foreclosure, Melissa gently suggested that we rent it out. In that, and in so many other ways, she keeps us untangled. I've always been a dreamer—sometimes a reckless one. Melissa makes sure that our dreams are corralled into an actual plan of action and that we don't go broke chasing them.

Lesson #12: Apologize

Melissa:

Eighteen years is a long time—and a long time to make mistakes. In my younger years, I was guilty of avoiding an official apology. Even now I find ways to apologize without saying, "I'm sorry." I have initiated sex as a means of apologizing. I have offered Kev some of my wings as a way to say "I'm sorry" without saying those two words. But you gotta learn how to say it. There's something very powerful and reconciliatory about saying, "I apologize. I was wrong."

The beautiful thing is that it's never too late to say "I'm sorry." Remember my regret that I cited in Lesson #3, "Seasons"? Years later, I apologized to Kevin for not quitting my job and going on tour with him. It wasn't about saying I was sorry for my choice. It was more about acknowledging that I hurt him, that my decision made him feel that I didn't believe in him. My apologizing at long last resonated with him, because he felt that I truly and finally understood the impact my actions had on him.

Apologize to your partner when you're wrong, even if it's something that happened in the past. It'll only strengthen the relationship and start the repair process.

Kevin:

I have messed up a lot. Consequently, I've gotten very used to saying, "I'm sorry." Practice makes perfect, as they say. Now

I'm a great apologizer. I do it so well and so often. Frankly, I'm a little surprised Melissa didn't learn earlier from me about how to do it.

Melissa:

That's because I never do anything wrong. I have nothing to apologize for.

Kevin:

Insert eye roll here.

Lesson #13: Intimacy

Melissa:

When most people think about intimacy, they think in terms of sex or physical affection. But intimacy can also refer to a connection that is created through emotional closeness, mental stimulation, or conversation. After eighteen years, I know for sure that for *me*, intimacy is a combination of all the above.

Here are my key takeaways about intimacy:

- At its core, intimacy is about feeling safe.
- All definitions of intimacy matter.
- Intimacy is an environment where you are confident enough to say no but vulnerable enough to say yes.

Kevin:

I used to think the word *intimates* was just JCPenney's slang for lingerie. You know, 'cause they were classy like that. But I have learned that it involves everything from sharing your fears to sharing your dreams, even sharing random thoughts that cross your mind.

I used to never share my fears with Melissa. I thought it made me look weak. I thought it would make them come true. Now I cry around her all the time. It's like once I stopped holding all that in, the floodgates opened. It taught me that vulnerability is not just reserved for pillow talk after sex. (Well, sometimes it is.) It's about being present with your partner and unafraid to be known by the person you love.

Sharing my fears has brought me and Melissa closer. Much of my life is shared on social media, on podcasts, and in stand-up. But there's a side of me that is reserved for only her. I have learned to give her access to parts of me that no one else has.

Lesson #14: Celebrate

Melissa:

Marriage is beautiful and deserves to be celebrated, but often we're too busy to stop and truly appreciate the milestones as they're happening. So, take the time to celebrate. Shine a light on the big accomplishments and precious moments that you are lucky enough to share.

Here are a few of my favorite celebrations we've had as a couple:

- On Valentine's Day, 2006, I was pregnant with Isaiah, and we had an appointment with my obstetrician. We had an ultrasound where we heard the heartbeat, which rang out loud, strong, and clear. I tear up thinking about that moment. Any fear I had about becoming a mom was immediately lifted. It was a beautiful moment where Kevin and I embraced our future. I had been terrified to become a parent, but suddenly in that moment, all was right with me. I knew I'd picked the right person to make a life with. As I cried, Kevin held my hand, and everything made sense.

- When we got our first "real" jobs, our starting salaries were $32,000 and $35,000 with *paid time off*! Mama, we made it! We were so excited! We didn't have money to spend on an actual celebration, but we called each other and shared our disbelief. That was celebration enough. There was nothing more exciting or grown up than PTO.

- Our first international trip together was a cruise to Jamaica. A cruise? Maaaaan, we thought we were grown-grown! That cruise was a celebration that our hard work had paid off and allowed us to vacation in the lap of luxury. In our twenties, no less!

- We also celebrate the smaller stuff: family outings at Mariners games, dinners with the boys, and Fredericks' family movie night with my world-famous chicken meatloaf.

- I know some people treat their anniversary as just another day. For me, it's not. It's a day we always celebrate. Even if we do a small dinner, we always take time to celebrate the fact that we made it another year.

Kevin:

As I write this, we are celebrating Melissa's birthday on a trip to St. Lucia. To be honest, this year we kinda wrapped our anniversary and her birthday celebrations into one trip, so we could sleep at night knowing we got two for the price of one. When I looked for pictures to post on Facebook for our anniversary, I was reminded of years three, five, and seven, and it seemed like ages ago.

This vacation spot is the most beautiful thing I've seen on God's green earth. I mean, the view is like something out of a movie. It's like *Jurassic Park* without the dinosaurs. Beautiful, lush mountains in the distance. Greenery everywhere we look. Birds chirping in the cloudless sky. Our hotel is built into the hillside, and the room has an open-air concept, with no walls between us and the outside.

Looking out at the view, it's such a far cry from my dungeon apartment where we started out. It feels like the best part of "till death do us part." We signed up for life together, no matter what, and while this trip to St. Lucia has been a dream come true, it's also a dream we never even dreamed. We were happy on our first cruise, in that interior stateroom on Royal Caribbean, and we would have been happy with that once more.

It is difficult to stay married. To be ever-changing yourself and to love a person who is also ever-changing require an amount of work that many of us underestimate. When Melissa and I mark making it through another year of marriage, you're darn right we are going to celebrate that. It's hard to score a touchdown, score a goal, and hit a home run. This trip was a trot around the bases combined with an end-zone dance.

Lesson #15: Everything Ain't for Everybody

Melissa:

Have you ever been advised not to tell family members when your spouse has upset you or disappointed you, because when y'all make up, you'll forgive your spouse but your mama will hold it against them till the end of time? No? Well, consider yourself advised. Not only have I learned to not share everything with my family, but I have also learned to create boundaries with social media. People sometimes say, "If you didn't post it, it didn't happen." I have rewritten it to say, "If you don't post it, it's more sacred." Precious moments happen between you and your spouse, whether you post them or not. In fact, *not* posting a moment you have with your spouse can make it even more precious.

Kevin and I once spent an entire date on our phones, documenting it for social media instead of being present with and focused on each other. I mean, talk about defeating the purpose! When I see couples out at a restaurant, sitting across from each other but on their phones, I know that Kevin and I have done the exact same thing. We might rationalize the behavior with "Our careers are dependent on social media activity," but the truth is, not every moment between the two of us is for public consumption. No one needs to know where you are and what you're doing at all times.

It took years for us to learn that everything ain't for everybody. Keep some things private, just for the two of you.

Kevin:

In the world of social media, people (and by *people,* I mean me) feel like we have to expose our whole selves online to be completely authentic. And I'm not just talking about Facebook, Twitter, and Instagram. Your friends and families don't require an all-access pass to your marriage. Some things are just for the two of you.

On the *Here's the Thing* podcast with my friends Angel Tanksley and Josh Gonzales, I talked about all the sex Melissa and I had on our vacation in Mexico. I went on and on, saying, "We did it everywhere, all throughout the day and night." Angel called Melissa while we were recording and ratted me out. Melissa was so upset. She explained that we need to be able to have experiences without my telling the world about them. She even said she's going to be less likely to do something if she fears it's going to end up as content.

For Melissa's birthday one year, I bought her a pair of sparkly, high-heeled $1,200 Christian Louboutin shoes. I was so excited to give them to her, and I remember how I recorded her opening them and posted it live on social media. To say that Melissa was nonplussed by the gift would be a gross understatement. Even our fans and followers noticed that Melissa was less than excited by the shoes. She didn't care. The problem wasn't the actual gift; it was the public display. The shoes, and the way I gave them to her, were more of a gift for myself and my ego. I was more interested in people I don't even know thinking and saying I'm a good husband than my own wife thinking the same thing.

Melissa and I have decided that certain things are just for us, our little secret. Not for the podcast, not for our families, not for our best friends. Not even something to come up later as a joke at a dinner party. Those little secrets have given us joy and allowed us to move freely as a couple.

Relationship Check-In

As we look back on the eighteen years of our marriage, we feel a whole host of emotions. The lessons we have learned ensure that we will be smarter and more thoughtful as we embark on the next eighteen. But we will make mistakes; that is a given. And those mistakes will lead to more lessons. The cycle will continue. But one thing is for sure: We will always champion marriage—ours and yours.

Here's our final relationship check-in:

- What are the lessons you have learned from your marriage?
- What are you learning together this year?
- What milestones or shared experiences can you celebrate today?

Notes

Introduction

1. 1 Corinthians 7:9.
2. See 2 Corinthians 12:7–9.

Chapter 1

1. "Funny Katt Williams Quotes," FunnyComedianQuotes.com, http://funnycomedianquotes.com/funny-katt-williams-jokes-and -quotes.html?p=2.
2. Juvenile, "Back That Azz Up," by Mannie Fresh, Lil Wayne, and Juvenile, track 13 on *400 Degreez,* Cash Money Records, 1998, https://genius.com/Juvenile-back-that-azz-up-lyrics.

Chapter 2

1. Alessia Cara, "Here," by Bobby Brass et al., track 2 on *Know-It-All,* Def Jam Recordings, 2015, https://genius.com/Alessia-cara -here-lyrics.
2. "*Madagascar* (2005): Quotes," IMDb, https://www.imdb.com/title/ tt0351283/quotes/?ref_=tt_trv_qu.
3. John Gottman and Nan Silver, *The Seven Principles for Making Marriage Work* (New York: Three Rivers Press, 1999), 160–61.

Chapter 3

1. See 1 Kings 11:1–3.
2. Quoted in Sandi Villarreal, "Their Generation Was Shamed by Purity Culture. Here's What They're Building in Its Place," *Sojourners,* March 7, 2019, https://sojo.net/interactive/their -generation-was-shamed-purity-culture-heres-what-theyre -building-its-place.
3. Emily Nagoski, *Come as You Are* (New York: Simon & Schuster, 2015), chap. 4.
4. Hebrews 13:4, ESV.
5. Laurie J. Watson, *Wanting Sex Again: How to Rediscover Your Desire and Heal a Sexless Marriage* (New York: Berkley Books, 2012), chap. 2.

Chapter 5

1. Alexandra Schwartz, "Love Is Not a Permanent State of Enthusiasm: An Interview with Esther Perel," *The New Yorker,* December 9, 2018, https://www.newyorker.com/culture/the-new -yorker-interview/love-is-not-a-permanent-state-of-enthusiasm-an -interview-with-esther-perel.

Chapter 6

1. Esther Perel, "Rethinking Infidelity: A Talk for Anyone Who Has Ever Loved," TED2015, March 2015, https://www.ted.com/talks/ esther_perel_rethinking_infidelity_a_talk_for_anyone_who_has _ever_loved/transcript?language=en.
2. "Home Rooms: Quotes," *The Wire,* September 24, 2006, https:// www.imdb.com/title/tt0763096/quotes/?ref_=tt_trv_qu.
3. Esther Perel, "Two Ways Couples Who Bounced Back Made It Happen," *Psychotherapy Networker,* https://www.psychotherapy networker.org/blog/details/1045/esther-perels-secret-to-weathering -an-affair.

Chapter 7

1. "The Junto Emotion Wheel," The Junto Institute, https://www
   .thejuntoinstitute.com/emotion-wheels.

Chapter 8

1. Melissa Pintor Carnagey, "8 Reasons Parents Avoid 'the Talks,'"
   Sex Positive Families, https://sexpositivefamilies.com/8-reasons
   -parents-avoid-the-talks.
2. Boston University Medical Center, "Italian Youths Who Drink
   with Meals Are Less Often Adult Problem-Drinkers,"
   ScienceDaily, August 20, 2010, https://www.sciencedaily.com/
   releases/2010/08/100819112224.htm.
3. See Genesis 38:6–10.

Chapter 9

1. "Glassblowing 101," Epiphany Studios, April 14, 2020, https://
   epiphanyglass.com/glassblowing-101.

Chapter 10

1. Mark 10:8.
2. Mark 10:9.
3. Narelle Storey, "Four Kinds of Love: Eros, Agape, Phileo, and
   Storge," Eros to Agape, August 9, 2012, https://fromerostoagape
   .wordpress.com/2012/08/09/eros-romantic-love-and-agape
   -unconditional-love.
4. Storey, "Four Kinds of Love."

Chapter 11

1. See Genesis 1:27; Psalm 139:14.

Chapter 12

1. Anita Baker, "Giving You the Best That I Got," *Giving You the Best That I Got,* Elektra, 1988, https://www.songfacts.com/lyrics/anita-baker/giving-you-the-best-that-i-got.

2. Proverbs 22:6, ESV.

About the Authors

KEVIN FREDERICKS is an NAACP Image Award nominated comedian, the founder of KevOnStage Studios, and a superstar on social media, posting hilarious content rooted in faith, family, and overall relatability for millions of followers every day. His work and commentary have been featured by *Good Morning America, Complex, Ebony, Newsweek, The Daily Beast,* and MSNBC.

kevonstage.com
Facebook.com/KevOnStage
Twitter: @KevOnStage
Instagram: @kevonstage

MELISSA FREDERICKS is a Los Angeles–based influencer dedicated to helping women become the best versions of themselves through honesty, transparency, and vulnerability. Melissa captivates audiences with talk of her personal journey of self-discovery and self-love, while challenging women to find themselves, lovingly accept their uniqueness, and realize their beauty and self-worth. Together she and Kevin are the founders of the *Love Hour* podcast, which has been downloaded millions of times to date.

mrskevonstage.com
Facebook.com/MrsKevOnStage
Twitter: @MrsKevOnStage
Instagram: @mrskevonstage

About the Type

This book was set in Sabon, a typeface designed by the well-known German typographer Jan Tschichold (1902–74). Sabon's design is based upon the original letter forms of sixteenth-century French type designer Claude Garamond and was created specifically to be used for three sources: foundry type for hand composition, Linotype, and Monotype. Tschichold named his typeface for the famous Frankfurt typefounder Jacques Sabon (c. 1520–80).